Baby Names
for the Girl

Published by
Lotus Press

Published by
Lotus Press

Baby Names
for the Girl

Vijaya Kumar

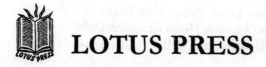
LOTUS PRESS

Lotus Press
4263/3, Ansari Road, Darya Ganj, New Delhi-2
Ph.: 30903912, 23290047
E-mail: lotus_press@sify.com

Baby Names for the Girl
© Lotus Press
Reprint 2004
ISBN 81-901912-3-3

LEICESTER CITY
LIBRARIES

X 840 39758x 1537	
MAGI	10·11·04
ANF	£ 2·99
929·44	

All rights are reserved. No part of this publication may be reproduced, stored in a retrieval system or transmitted, in any form or by any means, photocopying, recording or otherwise without prior written permission of the publisher.

Published by: Lotus Press, New Delhi.
Lasertypeset by: Jain Media Graphics, Delhi.
Printed at: Gyan Sagar, Delhi.

Preface

What's in a name? Everything! It is your name with which you are identified. All of us are interested in the meaning of our names.

When you are pregnant, you have so many things to decide and think about. Choosing the name for your baby is one of the most important things you will decide.

This is a book that tells you what you really want to know. Find a rare, uncommon and unusual name for your special baby! Or, find a common, popular or traditional name for your baby! With over 3,000 names to choose from, you are sure to find one that is as special as your baby.

This ultimate guide to baby names from India is entertaining and insightful, providing informative and interesting meanings, literal as well as figurative.

The names have been sourced from various books and texts.

Pronunciation
ā   as in *a*rm
ū   as in t*oo*
th as in *th*ermal
ṭh as in pa*th* (lesson)
ñ   as in gu*nn* (virtue)
ḍ   as in *d*id
ṭ   as in *t*ea

Ābhā: splendour, beauty, likeness

Abhidhā: name

Abhigyā: intelligent, ingenious

Abhilāshā: desire, wish

Abhirakshā: protector

Abhitā: fearless

Abhivibhā: illuminant

Abline: white

Achalā: earth, immovable

Acheerā: swift, prompt, brief, active

Achinā: carefree

Aḍaliā: refuge of God, just, noble.

Adarā: beauty

Aḍeline: of noble birth

Adhrishyā: invincible

Adhyā: beyond imagination

Adijā: of the mountain, an apsara's name

Adishyanti: invincible, sage Parashar's mother

Āditā: the first root

Aditi: perfection, freedom, safety, abundance

Aḍivā: pleasant, gentle

Adrijā: Parvati

Adrikā: small hill

Ādyā: first, excellent, earth, Durga

Aganjitā: the conqueror of fire

Āgneji: daughter of fire, Kuru's wife, daughter of Agni

Agrajā: born first, elder daughter

Ahalyā: agreeable, sage Gautama's wife

Ahanā: one who cannot be killed, immortal, day-born

Ahi: heaven and earth conjoined

Ahladitā: delighted

Āhuti: summoning, offering

Ahwānā: call, summon

Aiḍa: joyful, helper, reward

Aileen: light, green meadow

Aikshvāki: very sweet

Aishwaryā: wealth, glory, fame

Ajātā: eternal, another name for earth

Ājāni: of noble birth

Ajarā: ever youthful, river Saraswati

Ajathyā: yellow jasmine

Ajayā: unconquerable

Ajeerā: quick, agile, Durga

Ajitā: unconquerable

Ākaliki: lightning

Ākānkshā: desire, wish

Ākāshdeepā: a lamp in the sky, bright

Ākāshgangā: the Milky Way, the celestial Ganga

Ākāshi: all-pervading, atmosphere

Akhilā: intelligent

Akifā: devoted, dedicated

Ākrānti: valour, force

Ākriti: form, shape

Akshamālā: a rosary of Rudraksha seeds

Akshayā: undecaying, the goddess of earth

Akshāyani: undying

Akshi: existence, abode, possession, eye

Akshimanā: ruby

Akshiti: that which is imperishable

Akupārā: free, independent

Ākuti: intention

Alakā: trees, girl

Alaknandā: young girl, the celestial Ganga

Alametā: extremely intelligent

Alamelu: very sportive, extremely merry

Ālāpini: a bite

Alimā: wise, learned

Alishā: stately, grand

Āliyā: high, exalted

Allanā: fair

Alpanā: glad, delighted

Alvinā: noble friend

Amalā: pure, shining, Lakshmi

Amaranganā: celestial damsel

Amari: eternal

Amāris: child of the moon

Amartā: immortal

Amati: beyond intellect, splendour, time, lustre

Ambā: mother, a god, woman

Ambālikā: mother, a sensitive person

Ambar: sky

Ambhini: water-born

Ambikā: mother, compassionate, loving

Ambujākshi: lotus-eyed, with beautiful eyes

Amelia: industrious

Aminyā: pure, chaste

Amirā: princess, rich, grand

Amishā: guileless

Amiti: boundless, divine

Amiyā: nectar, full of tenderness

Āmodini: fragrance, famous

Āmohanikā: fragrance

Amoghā: productive, unerring

Amrishā: genuine, real

Amritā: immortal, nectar-like, goddess

Amritāmālini: with an everfresh garland, Durga

Amshulā: bright, radiant

Anabhrā: clear-minded

Anadhikā: without a superior

Anādyā: immortal, divine, an apsara

Anāgā: sinless, a river

Analā: without a blemish

Anāmikā: nameless yet full of virtues, ring finger

Ānamrā: humble, modest, propitious

Anan: clouds

Ānandamayi: full of bliss

Anandanā: happy

Ānandi: bestower of pleasure, Gauri

Anantā: eternal, divine

Anantikā: simple

Anantyā: without an equal

3

Ananyā: sole, unique, peerless

Anasuyā: without envy or spite

Anatā: straight, erect

Ānati: modest, humble, respectful

Ānavi: kind, humane

Aneemā: wife of Lord Ganesh

Aneeshā: without night

Anganā: a beautiful woman

Angārita: blossom of kinshuk tree, a river

Angeerā: celestial, divine, beyond description

Anguri: finger, finger ring

Anhati: gift

Anindā: beyond reproach

Anisā: friendly

Anitā: guileless, a leader, grace

Anjalā: unscorched

Anjali: hollow formed by joining hands together

Anjanā: dusky, swarthy

Anjanam: night, fire, jet black

Anjashi: honest, not dark, deceitless

Anji: blesser

Anjini: blessed

Anjori: moonlight

Anjunā: name of Hanuman's mother

Ankitā: with auspicious marks

Ankolikā: personifier of love and respect

Ankushi: one who exercises restraint

Annabelle: joy

Annadā: bestower of food, Durga

Annapurnā: bestower of food to the utmost, Durga

Anokhi: unique

Anomā: illustrious

Anshu: sunbeam

Anshumālā: halo, as glorious as the sun, a garland of rays

Anshumati: resplendent, wise, bearer of rays

4

Āntikā: elder sister

Anubhā: one who follows glory, lightning

Anuchārā: well behaved, an apsara, devoted to learning

Anugā: a companion, a follower, an apsara

Anujā: younger sister

Anukā: backbone, support

Anukampā: kindness, tenderness, pity

Anulā: gentle, tamed

Anunitā: prayer

Anutānkshā: desire, wish

Anutā: gentle, agreeable

Anulekhā: a follower of destiny

Anuli: respected, homage

Anumoditā: delighted, applauded

Anūnā: superior, entire, an apsara

Anuneetā: learned, wise, respected

Anupā: unique, unequalled, river bank

Anupallavi: tender, fragrant, young, soft like a petal

Anupamā: unique, matchless, rare

Anurādhā: bestower of welfare

Anurakti: love, devotion, affection

Anuranjanā: love, affection

Anurimā: fond of, attached

Anusarā: full of desires

Anushobhini: shining, dignified, illuminant

Anushree: glorious, famous

Anuvindā: discoverer, finder

Anvadhyā: goddess

Anvitā: linked to, understood, reached by the mind

Anyā: that which is not exhaustible

Apārā: boundless, divine, unequalled

Aparnā: without leaves, Parvati

Apekshitā: desired, expected, awaited

Āpti: abundance, fortune, fulfilment

Apūrvā: incomparable, extraordinary

Ārādhanā: worship, prayer

Ārādhitā: worshipped, a receiver of devotion

Arajā: clean, pure, virtuous

Aranyani: Parvati

Ārati: offering prayer, spiritual, venerated

Aravindini: fragrant, beautiful, auspicious

Archanā: propitiated, worship

Archis: flame, illuminating, ray of light

Arhanā: honoured, worship, venerated

Arhantikā: worshipper, one who shuns violence

Ariktā: satisfied, abundant

Ariprā: spotless, virtuous, divine

Arishṭṭā: safe, unhurt

Arjā: pure, virtuous, divine

Arkajā: daughter of sun god

Ārleen: pledge

Ārohi: positive, progressive, ascending

Arpanā: auspicious, sacred, venerated

Arpitā: offered, delivered, entrusted, surrendered

Arthanā: entreaty

Artikā: elder sister

Arujā: daughter of Sun god

Arukshitā: not dry, supple, young, soft, tender

Arunā: red, life-giving, passionate, an apsara

Arundhati: fidelity

Aruṇi: ruddy, dawn, gold, passionate, illuminating, sacred

Aruṇikā: tawny red, bright, passionate

Aruṇimā: reddish glow, sacred dawn glow

Arūpā: formless, unbounded, divine

Arvanti: nymph, mare

Āryā: a noble lady, worshipped, respected

Āryaki: honoured, respected, Durga

Āshā: desire, wish, space, region

Āshāli: liked by all

Āsheeshā: blessed, hope

Ashley: ash-tree

Ashmaki: strong and subtle

Ashokā: without sorrow, blossom of Ashoka tree

Ashwākinī: strong, swift

Ashviktā: a small mare

Ashwini: wealthy, a swift mover

Asitā: unbound, the dark one

Asmitā: renunciation

Āsthā: care, hope, support, confidence, consideration

Atibālā: goddess

Atiki: overflowing, excelling

Atimoda: very fragrant, very happy, jasmine

Ātyreji: receptacle of glory

Atūhā: fragrant, jasmine

Auḍrey: noble, strength

Aureliā: golden

Avabhā: brilliant, bright

Avanati: humble, modest

Avanti: endless, modest

Avantikā: very modest

Avenā: oats

Avichalā: everlasting

Avishi: not poisonous, heaven, earth, nectar-like

Avishyā: desire, full of ardour

Āyati: posterity, dignity, majesty

Ayeshā: Prophet Mohammed's favourite wife

Ayodhikā: calm, peace-loving

Azaleā: flower, democracy

Azizāh: beloved, precious, rare

B

Babette: consecrated to God

Babita: born in the first quarter of an astrological day

Bachendri: sense of speech, tongue

Bādarāyani: pure, young, new, perfume

Bāgeshree: beauty, prosperity

Bāhair: beautiful, delicate

Bahār: spring, beauty, glory

Bahudā: giving bountifully

Bahulikā: multiplied, manifold, magnified, a multifaceted personality

Bahumati: extremely knowledgeable, a scholar patient, watchful, circumspect

Bakulā: like a crane, blossom of Bakula tree, patient, watchful, circumspect

Bakulikā: small blossom of Bakula tree

Bakulitā: decked with Bakula blossoms

Bālā: girl, jasmine, young child

Baladā: bestower of strength

Bālasandhyā: early twilight, dawn

Bālini: strong, Ashwini, constellation

Bandhini: binder, bond, bound

Bandhurā: charming, lovely

Barakhā: white one

Barhiñā: decked with peacock feathers

Basanti: of the spring, excitement

Basimā: smiling

Basudā: earth

Beenā: harp

Bekuri: playing a musical instrument, an apsara

Belā: jasmine creeper

Belli: companion

Benazir: matchless, with no equal, peerless

Beniyāz: carefree, with no wants

Bernaḍine: bold as bear

Beṭṭinā: consecrated to God

Beulā: married

Bhadrā: beautiful, fair, fortunate, prosperous, gentle, gracious, auspicious

Bhadrāvati: noble

Bhadrikā: a noble woman, virtuous, auspicious, beautiful

Bhāgavanti: fortunate, shareholder

Bhagyashree: goddess of fortune, Lakshmi

Bhairavi: Durga

Bhāmā: splendour, light

Bhāmini: radiant, beautiful, glorious

Bhānavi: shining like the sun, sacred, illuminating

Bhānu: light, beautiful, virtuous, enlightened

Bhānujā: daughter of Sun god

Bhānumati: luminous, famous, enlightening, beautiful

Bhānupriyā: beloved of Sun god

Bhānushree: as glorious as the sun

Bharani: fulfiller

Bharati: Saraswati

Bhāravā: pleasing sound, agile

Bhārgavi: descendant of Bhrigu, radiant, charming, beautiful, Lakshmi, Parvati

Bhāshi: bright, lustrous, illusory

Bhāswati: luminous, splendid

Bhāti: loved by all, splendour, perception, light, knowledge

Bhattarikā: noble lady, sacred, venerated, virtuous, Durga

Bhaumā: of the earth, steady

Bhavadā: giving life

Bhāvajā: boon of the heart, sentimental,

sincere, beautiful, compassionate

Bhāvana: feeling, thought, meditation, feeling, imagination

Bhavāni: consort of Bhava, Parvati

Bhavanikā: living in a castle

Bhavanti: now, becoming, new, charming

Bhāviki: sentimental, emotional, real, natural

Bhāvilā: good, worthy

Bhāvini: inducing emotions, noble, beautiful, illustrious, sensitive, loving

Bhāvukā: sentimental, emotional, real, natural

Bhavyā: magnificent, beautiful, tranquil, worthy, Parvati

Bhavyakeerti: very wise, with magnificent fame

Bhogadā: bestower of worldly pleasures and happiness

Bhogavati: Ganga

Bhogyā: an object of enjoyment, precious stone

Bhomirā: from the earth, life-giving, tolerant

Bhrāji: lustre, splendour, fame, glory

Bhrami: whirlwind, whirlpool

Bhūmayi: full of existence, from the earth

Bhūmijā: born of earth, Sita

Bhūshā: ornament, precious, wealthy, much loved

Bhuvā: fire, earth

Bhuvanā: omnipresent, earth

Bijli: lightning, bright, illuminating, glorious

Bimbā: as glorious as the sun or moon

Bimbini: pupil (of the eye)

Binā: cute, melodious, harmonious

Bindiyā: a small dot

Bindu: mark, symbol, alphabet, truth, pearl, origin, subtle, absolute, divine, drop

Binotā: harp

Bisālā: sprout, bud, young, short, a child

Blossom: flower, lovely

Bodhanā: the awakening, knowledge, intellect

Brāhmaṇī: life of Brahma, wise, intelligent, sacred

Bree: broth

Brenḍā: fiery hill, sword blade

Brennā: raven maid

Brettā: from Britain

Briānā: strong

Brice: quick-moving

Bridgeṭ: resolute, strength, saint

Brietta: strong

Brinā: protector

Brindā: surrounded by many, Radha

Briṭes: strength

Brook: stream

Burḍeṭṭe: small bird

Camillā: freedom girl

Carlottā: strong

Cary: honest, shy

Casey: brave, watchful

Chāhanā: desire, affection

Chāhat: desire

Chaitāli: of the mind, with a sharp memory

Chaitri: born in spring, tender and fresh like a new blossom, ever-happy

Chakore: shining, content, a bird

Chakrikā: Lakshmi

Chakshani: illuminating to the eyes, illuminating

Chameli: jasmine

Champā: soothing, flower of the champaka tree

Champikā: small champa blossom

Chanasyā: delighting

Chanchalā: restless, lightning, a river, Lakshmi

Chandā: passionate, wrathful, moon

Chandalikā: Durga

Chandanā: sandalwood, fragrant, cool, auspicious

Chandaneekā: a small sandalwood tree

Chandikā: Durga

Chāndini: silver, moonlight, cool, luminous, fair

Chandrā: moon

Chandrabālā: daughter of Moon god, as beautiful as the moon

Chandrabindu: crescent moon

Chandrahāsā: with a beautiful smile

Chandrajā: daughter of Moon god, moonbeam

Chandrajyoti: moonlight

Chandrakāntā: wife of Moon god

Chandrakriti: moon-shaped

Chandrāli: moonbeam

Chandramālā: garland of the moon, of great beauty, aura of the moon

Chandrāni: wife of Moon god

Chandraprabhā: moon-beam

Chandrasheelā: stone of the moon, calm, soothing

Chandrashree: divine moon, tranquil, beautiful, charming

Chandrashubhrā: lit by the moon, as fair as the moon

Chandratārā: moon and stars conjoined, eye-catching

Chāndri: moonlight, cord, soothing, fair

Chandrikā: moonlight, illuminant, cool, soothing, jasmine creeper

Chandrimā: moonlight

Chāndvati: Durga

Charchitā: repeating a word, fragrant, attractive

Charani: wanderer, a bird

Charshani: active, swift, moonlight, saffron, intelligence

Chāru: beautiful

Chāruchitrā: beautiful

Chārulatā: beautiful vine

Chārumati: wise, intelligent, enlightened

Chārunetrā: with beautiful eyes

Chārusheelā: beautiful jewel

Chārutamā: most beautiful

Chāruvāki: with a sweet tongue, pleasant

Chāruveni: a beautiful braid

Chāruvi: splendour

Chārvāngi: with a beautiful body

Chaturi: clever, skilful, wise

Chaturikā: clever, skilful

Chavi: reflection, image, ray of light, image, splendour

Chāyā: shade, shadow, reflection, beauty, colour, shine, likeness

Chelanā: of consciousness nature

Chelsea: river, landing place

13

Chetaki: perceptible, jasmine

Chetana: intelligence, consciousness, wisdom, life, knowledge, sense

Chitpara: beyond thought, indescribable

Chitra: beautiful, picture, ornament, sky, painting, heaven, worldly illusion, conspicuous, an apsara

Chitrajyoti: luminous, shining brightly

Chitrali: wonderful woman, friend of the strange

Chitramaya: worldly illusion, strange manifestation

Chitramayi: full of wonders, like a picture

Chitrangi: with a charming body

Chitrani: Ganga

Chitrashree: with divine beauty

Chitravati: decorated

Chitrini: endowed with excellence, talented, brightly ornamented

Chitrita: ornamented, painted

Chitta: intellectual, spiritual, thoughtful

Chitti: thought, understanding, devotion

Chudala: forming the crest, an apsara

Chumba: kiss, adorable person

Colleen: girl

Columbia: dove

Corinna: maiden

Corliss: cheerful and generous

D

Daisy: pearl, flower

Daksha: earth

Dakshakanyā: an able daughter

Dakshāyani: emerging from fire, golden ornament, daughter of a perfect being

Dakshayi: perfect

Dakshinā: donation to priest or god, able, fit, right-handed

Dalajā: honey, produced from petals

Dale: valley

Dalini: Durga

Dāmā: suppressor, wealthy, self-restrained

Damayanti: self-restrained, subduer of men

Dāmini: lightning

Dampā: lightning

Dānti: patience, self-restraint

Danu: high-pitched

Ḍaphne: laurel

Darpanikā: a small mirror

Darshanā: intellect, virtue

Darshatashree: of apparent beauty

Darshayāmini: night worthy of watching, new-moon night

Darshini: worth looking at, Durga

Dattādevi: goddess of gifts

Datti: a gift

Davani: fire

Davini: lightning

Dayā: compassion, sympathy

Dayanā: compassionate

Dayānvitā: surrounded by mercy, full of mercy

Dayitā: worthy of compassion, beloved, cherished

Debbie: bee

Deepā: illuminated, enlightening

Deepākshi: bright-eyed

Deepāli: a row of lights

Deepana: illuminating, kindler, in flames, passion

Deepani: exciting, stimulating, illuminating

Deepanjali: a prayer lamp

Deepavati: earth

Deepika: a small lamp, light, moonlight

Deepshikha: flame of lamp

Deepta: illuminated, blazing, bright, brilliant

Deepti: radiance, brightness, enlightening, illuminating

Deeraghika: tall girl, oblong lake

Deshna: gift, offering

Devaduni: Ganga

Devagiri: divine knowledge

Devaki: divine, pious, glorious

Devalata: double jasmine

Devalekha: divine line, celestial beauty

Devamala: divine garland, an apsara

Devamati: Godly-minded, virtuous, venerated

Devananda: joy of the gods, an apsara

Devashree: divine goddess, Lakshmi

Devasmita: with a divine smile

Devata: music personified

Devayani: chariot of the gods, endowed with divine powers, divine affluence

Devayoni: divine creation

Deveshi: chief of the goddesses, Durga

Devika: Yudhishtra's wife

Dhamini: pipe, tube

Dhanada: bestowing wealth

Dhanarati: containing wealth

Dhanashree: goddess of wealth

Dhanishttha: dwelling in wealth, very wealthy

Dhanu: sage Kashyap's wife

Dhanvanya: oasis, jungle treasure

Dhanya: virtuous, bestowing wealth, good

Dharā: supporter, earth, a gold mass

Dhārāni: holding, possessing, bearing

Dharmini: pious, religious, virtuous, perfume

Dhātreyikā: supporter, nurse, companion

Dheeshanā: vessel for soma, knowledge, speech, hymn, intelligence

Dhenukā: milch cow

Dhikshā: initiation, consecration, dedication

Dhitā: a daughter

Dhiti: idea, wisdom, reflection, intention, prayer

Dhritavati: calm, steady, a river

Dhriti: firmness, constancy, joy, resolution

Dhritimati: resolute, steadfast

Dhūlikā: pollen of flowers

Dhun: wealth

Dhuti: splendour, majesty, lustre, light

Dhyeyā: ideal, aim

Dinika: sun

Dinumati: Gomati river

Dipakalikā: flame of a lamp

Dipakshit: bright-eyed

Dipnā: glitter, shine

Diprā: radiant, shining, flaming

Dishā: direction, region

Dishtti: direction, auspicious, good fortune, joy

Diti: glow, splendour, light, brightness, beauty

Divijā: born of the sky, celestial, heaven-born, goddess

Divyā: divine, charming, heavenly, celestial

Divyagandhā: with divine fragrance

Divyajyoti: divine light

Divyakriti: of divine form, beautiful

Dolly: gift of God

Dory: golden-haired

Drishikā: good looking

Druhi: daughter

Druti: softened, tender

Duā: blessing, benediction

Dulāri: lovable

Dumati: with bright intellect, a river

Dureshwari: goddess

Durgā: unapproachable, goddess of the universe

Durvaswati: offering worship, enjoying worship

Dyotanā: illuminating, shining

Dyotani: splendour, brightness

Dyukshā: celestial

Dyumayi: full of brightness

Dyuthi: shining, bright

Dyuvadhū: celestial woman, an apsara

Ebony: dark beauty

Eḍānā: zealous, fiery

Eḍḍā: rich

Edhā: prosperity, joy

Eḍonā: rejuvenation

Edsel: rich

Eḍwinā: feminine form of Edwin

Ekā: one and only, matchless, firm, Durga

Ekachandrā: the only moon, the best one

Ekajā: only child

Ekākini: alone

Ekamati: concentrated

Ekānanshā: new moon

Ekangikā: of sandalwood, auspicious, frequent, fair, dear to the gods

Ekantā: beautiful, devoted to one

Ekāntikā: devoted to a single intention

Ekaparnā: single-leafed, residing on a leaf

Ekāvali: a string of pearls

Ekishā:one goddess, primal goddess

Ekshikā: eye

Ektā: unity

Ekyastikā: single string of pearls

Elā: earth, born of earth

Ellā: beautiful

Elokshi: hair black as cardamom creeper

Elvā: elf

Enā: doe, black antelope

Enākshi: doe-eyed

Eni: deer, spotted, flowing stream

Erakā: hard grass

Erikā: ever powerful

Erin: peace

Eshā: desire, wish, intention

Eshanikā: fulfilling desire, goldsmith's balance

Eshikhā: achiever of objective, arrow, dart

Eshitā: wanted, yearning

Esmereldā: green gemstone

Etā: shining, flowing

Etahā: shining

Eti: arrival

Eulaliā: fair of speech

Evadnā: fortunate

Evelinā: youth

Evelyn: lively, pleasant

F

Faihā: expanse, aromatic, perfumed

Faihāh: perfume, fragrance

Fainan: one with luxurious hair

Faizā: successful

Fakeehā: cheerful

Fakhirā: splendid, elegant

Fakhr: pride

Fakhtā: dove

Falaq: break of dawn

Falnā: famous, prosper

Fanhanā: female artist

Faqihā: well-versed in law, theologian

Farāh: joy, happiness, gaiety

Farhanā: happy

Faranā: famous, glorious

Faridā: sole, different, large pearl

Farihan: happy, woman

Farilatā: betel leaf

Farrāh: beautiful, wild ass

Faryā: friend

Farzi: queen (in chess, game)

Farzin: wise, intelligent, chess queen

Fasāh: shining in splendour

Fasanā: tale, myth, famous

Fatāt: a young maid

Fatimā: Prophet Muhammed's daughter

Fātin: captivating

Fazanā: intelligent

Fideliā: faithful

Fionā: white

Firzān: chess queen

Fisā: peacock

Flaviā: yellow

Foolrani: flower queen

Frashmi: prosperity

Frayashti: worship, praise

Freyā: dear, beloved

Freyanā: cherished
Friedā: peace
Frohar: angel

Fulmati: goddess
Fulnā: gladden, to make
one proud

Gabhasti: ray, moonbeam, sunbeam

Gagandeepikā: lamp of the sky, sun

Gagansindhu: celestial Ganga, ocean of the sky

Gail: gay, lively

Gajrā: garland of flowers

Gamati: with a flexible mind

Gambhāri: sky-reaching

Gamin: with a graceful gait

Gandhā: fragrant

Gandhajā: of fragrant perfume

Gandhalatā: fragrant creeper

Gandhāli: perfumed

Gandhālikā: fragrant, an apsara

Gandhārikā: preparing perfume

Gāndharvi: speech of celestial

Gandhavadhu: fragrant maiden

Gandhavaruni: with perfumed juice

Gandhavati: sweetly scented, earth, wine

Gāndhini: fragrant

Gangā : swift flowing

Gangikā: like the Ganga, pure like the Ganga

Ganjan: excelling, conquering, surpassing

Gannikā: counted of value, jasmine

Gārgi: water-holding vessel, churn

Garimā: grace, sublimity, divinity, greatness

Gāthikā: song

Gauhar: pearl

Gaunikā: jasmine, valuable

Gaurangi: fair, the colour of cow

Gauri: fair, brilliant, beautiful, jasmine

Gaurikā: like Gauri, Shiva

Gautami: dispeller of darkness

Gavah: stars of heaven

Gāyantikā: singing

Gāyatri: *Vedic* mantra or chant

Gāyatrini: the singer of the *Sama Veda* hymns

Geerā: speech, song, *Vedic* hymn, voice, language, Saraswati

Geeradevi: goddess of speech

Geetā: song, poem, lyric

Gitāli: lover of song

Geetānjali: devotional offering of a hymn

Geetashree: the divine Gita

Geeti: song

Geetikā: a short song

Geshā: singer

Ghanānjani: with colleriums as black as the clouds, Durga

Ghanavallikā: creeper of the clouds, lightning

Ghazal: lyric poem

Ghoshā: resounding, fame, proclamation

Ghoshinī: famed, proclaimed

Gilḍā: God's servant

Gughari: belled bracelet

Ghūrnikā: one who whirls

Giribālā: daughter of the mountain, Parvati

Giridevi: Saraswati

Girijā: daughter of the mountain

Girikā: mountain summit

Girikarnī: mountain lotus

Girikamīkā: earth, mountains as vessels for seeds

Girimallikā: mountain creeper, a flower

Girinandini: daughter of the mountain, Parvati, Ganga

Girindramohini: beloved of the lord of the mountains, Parvati

Gireeshā: lady of the mountains, Parvati

Gireshmā: summer

Girisutā: daughter of the mountain, Parvati

Girni: praise, celebrity

Gitāli: lover of song

Godāvari: granting water, bringer of prosperity, a river

Godetā: name of a flower

Gojā: born amidst rays, born in the earth

Goḷḍie: gold

Gomati: rich in cattle, milky, a river

Gomedā: respecter of cows, beryl

Gopabālā: daughter of a cowherd

Gopajā: daughter of cowherd

Gopāli: protector of cows, cowherdess, an apsara

Gopi: herdswoman, milkmaid of Krishna

Gopikā: herdswoman, cow protector, Radha

Gorochanā: yellow pigment, beautiful and virtuous woman

Grashiā: flavour, grace

Grihiñi: mistress of the house

Gulfroze: beautiful like a flower

Gulikā: anything round, a pearl

Gulmiñi: a creeper, clustering

Gulnār: pomegranate flower

Guñajā: daughter of virtue

Guñamayā: endowed with virtues

Guñāvarā: virtuous, meritorious, an apsara

Guñavati: virtuous

Guñaveeñā: virtuous

Guñchā: blossom, bud

Guñchalā: bunch of flowers

Guñitā: virtous, proficient

Gunjan: humming, a cluster of flowers

Gunjikā: humming, meditation

Gumikā: well woven, garland, necklace

Gupti: protecting, preserving

Gurnikā: wife of a teacher

Gūrti: praise, approval

Garudā: guru-given

Gurudeepā: lamp of the grace

Gurumeetā: friend of the guru

Gurusharnā: in the guru's protection

Gurwanti: virtuous, talented

Gwen: white, fair

26

Hādiyā: guide

Haifā: slender

Haimā: of the snow, golden, Parvati, Ganga

Haimavati: possessor of snow

Haimi: golden

Hairanyavati: possessing gold

Halā: earth, liquor, water, a female friend

Halipriyā: beloved of Vishnu

Hameedā: praiseworthy

Hamrā: red, fair lady

Hanan: mercy

Hansagāmini: as graceful as a swan

Hansanādini: slender-waisted, graceful gait, cuckoo-voiced

Hansanandini: daughter of a swan

Hansaveṇi: swan-like braid, with a beautiful braid, Saraswati

Hansi: swan

Hansikā: swan

Hansini: swan, goose

Hanum: woman, maiden

Haramālā: garland of Shiva

Harapriyā: beloved of Shiva, Parvati

Hārāvali: garland of pearls

Hardikā: sincere

Hari: reddish-brown, tawny

Haribālā: daughter of Vishnu

Haridrā: turmeric

Harikāntā: dear to Vishnu, Lakshmi

Harikiṇā: engrossed in Hari

Harileenā: merged in Vishnu

Harimālā: garland of Vishnu

Harinākshi: doe-eyed

Hariṇi: doe, gazelle, green, yellow jasmine, an apsara

Harimani: emerald

Haripriyā: dear to Vishnu, Lakshmi, earth, basil

Harishree: wonderfully golden, blessed with soma

Haritālikā: goddess of fertility, bringer of greenery

Hareeti: green, verdant, tawny

Harnyā: house, mansion, palace

Haroshit: happy, joyful

Harshalā: pleased

Harshaveenā: a lute that delights

Harshi: happy, joyful

Harshitā: full of joy

Harshumati: filled with joy

Hasanti: one who delights, jasmine

Hāsavati: full of laughter

Hasikā: in bloom, smiling, causing laughter

Hāsini: delightful, an apsara

Hasnā: beautiful

Hasnat: smiling, radiant, blooming

Hasrā: laughing woman, apsara

Hastakamatā: with lotus in hand, Lakshmi

Hasthā: star

Hasumati: always laughing

Havishmati: offering in sacrifices

Hayā: modesty

Hayānanā: yogini

Hāyati: flame

Hayi: desire, wish

Haylee: from the hay meadow

Hazel: a tree with nuts, commander

Heerā: diamond, Lakshmi

Hemā: golden, earth, handsome, a river

Hemabhā: looking like gold

Hemākshi: golden-eyed

Hemalatā: golden vine, yellow jasmine

Hemamālā: golden garland

Hemamālini: garland with gold

Hemangi: golden-bodied

Hemangini: with a golden body

Hemāni: of gold, as precious as gold, Parvati

Hemanti: of winter

Hemapushpikā: with small golden flowers, yellow jasmine

Hemarāgini: coloured gold, turmeric

Hemavamā: golden complexioned

Hemāvati: possessing gold, Parvati, mountain stream

Hemayuthikā: golden, woven, yellow jasmine

Himā: snow, night, winter

Himajā: daughter of snow, Parvati

Himalini: snow-covered

Himāni: snow, glacier, avalanche, Parvati

Himarashmi: white light, cool-rayed, moon, moonlight

Himashailajā: born of snow, Parvati

Himashwetā: as white as snow

Himasutā: daughter of snow, fair, calm, Parvati

Himi: snow

Hinā: fragrance, myrtle vine

Hiranyā: golden

Hiranyadā: giver of gold, earth

Hityashi: well-wisher

Hiyā: heart

Holly: plant with red berries

Honey: sweet

Hoor: fairy of paradise

Hotrā: invocation

Hridayhari: bewitching

Iḍā: this moment, intelligence, earth as food-bestower, insight, prosperous

Iḍikā: belonging to this moment, earth

Iḍiti: one who praises

Iditri: one who appreciates

Ihā: desire, wish, activity, effort

Ihitā: desired

Ijyā: gift, charity, worship

Ikshā: sight

Ihsheñyā: deserving to be seen

Ikshitā: seen, visible

Ikshu: sweetness

Ikshudā: giving wishes, bringing joy

Ikshugandhā: fragrant, as sweet smelling as sugarcane

Ikshutā: bringer of sweetness, wish-granting

Ikshulatā: creeper of sweetness

Ikshumati: one who is sweet

Ikshumālini: a sweet person

Ikshumālavi: a person who is sweet

Ikshuvāri: sugarcane juice, the sea of syrup

Ilā: earth, prayers, stream of praise, offering refreshment, recreation, mother, teacher, priestess, speech

Ilākshi: eye of the earth, hub of the earth

Ilāvilā: having insight, scholar, praise

Ilakā: small form of earth

Ileshā: queen of the earth

Ilhinā: highly intelligent

Ilikā: of earth, corporeal

Ilishā: queen of the earth

Ilvikā: protector of the earth

Imān: faith, belief

Impanā: sweet-voiced

Inākshi: sharp-eyed

Indali: to attain power

Indeevaraprabhā: light of the blue lotus

Indeevarini: collection of blue lotuses

Indira: bestower of power, bestower of prosperity, Lakshmi

Indrākshi: eyes like Indra

Indrāni: Indra's wife

Indraneelikā: as blue as Indra

Indrashakti: energy of Indra

Indratā: the power and majesty of Indra

Indrāyani: wife of Indra

Indu: a bright drop, soma, moon, camphor

Indubhavā: emerging from the moon

Indujā: daughter of the moon, Narmada river

Indukakshā: moon's radiating circle, orbit of the moon

Indukala: a part of the moon

Indukalika: a small part of the moon

Indukamala: white lotus

Indukānta: beloved of the moon, night

Indulekhā: a digit of the moon

Indumati: full moon, fair, calm, healing

Induratnā: jewel of the moon, pearl

Induvadanā: with a moon-like face

Inikā: earth in a small form

Ipsā: desire, wish

Ipsitā: desired, wished for

Irā: earth, speech, water, nourishment, refreshment

Irajā: daughter of the wind, primal water

Irāmā: happiness of the earth

Irāvati: clouds, full of milk or water

Irijayā: victorious wind

Irikā: a small form of earth

Isar: eminence

Ishā: power, faculty, dominion, Durga

Ishānā: sovereign, Durga

Ishani: possessing, ruling

Ishānikā: belonging to the north-east

Ishikā: painter's brush, pen for auspicious writing

Ishnā: ardent desire

Ishitkā: desired, greatness, superiority

Ishtā: that which is worshipped through sacrifice

Ishtarā: dearer

Ishttu: desire, wish

Ishukā: arrow, like an arrow, an apsara

Ishwari: goddess

Israt: affectionate

Itarā: another

Itkilā: full of fragrance

Iyā: pervading

J

Jabakusum: flower of meditation, beloved of Krishna

Jabālā: possessor of a herd of goats, a young cowherdess

Jadambā: mother of the world, Durga

Jagadgauri: fairest of the universe, Parvati

Jagadhātri: universe sustainer, Parvati, Saraswati

Jagajyoti: earth, creator of the world

Jagandāmbikā: with mother of the universe, Durga

Jaganmātā: mother of the world, Durga, Lakshmi

Jaganmohini: Durga

Jagatārini: saviour of the world

Jagatgauri: beauty of the universe

Jagati: of the universe, heaven and hell conjoined, earth

Jagavi: born of the universe

Jāgriti: alert, attentive, not extinguishable, fire, soma

Jāhnavi: earth-born, Ganga

Jaijaiwanti: full of victory, a song of victory

Jailekhā: a record of victory, victorious many times

Jaimālā: garland of victory

Jaimān: victorious

Jaiprabhā: light of victory

Jaipriyā: beloved of victory

Jaisheelā: character of victory, one who is habitually victorious

Jaisudhā: nectar of victory, sweet taste of victory

Jaitvati: bearer of victory, victorious

Jaivanti: long lived, being victorious

Jaivati: winning, being victorious

Jalā: full of water, charity

Jalabālā: daughter of the water, nymph, Lakshmi

Jalabālikā: daughter of the water, lightning as daughter of cloud

Jaladhijā: daughter of the ocean, Lakshmi

Jalahāsini: smile of water, wife of Krishna

Jalajā: born of the water, Lakshmi

Jalajākshi: lotus-eyed

Jalajātā: born of the water, lotus

Jalajini: a group of lotuses

Jalakāntā: beloved of water, ocean, wind

Jalakusumā: flower of water, lotus

Jalalatā: creeper of water, wave

Jalāmbikā: mother of water, well

Jalandharā: water bearer

Jalaneeli: as blue as water, water nymph

Jalapriyā: dear to water, a bird

Jalapushpā: water lily

Jalārnavā: ocean of water

Jallatā: stream, wave

Jāmā: daughter

Jambālini: maiden of water

Jamilā: beautiful

Jānā: God's greatest gift, fruit harvest

Janabālikā: very bright, lightning

Jānaki: daughter of Janaka

Janashruti: folklore

Janeshṭhā: desired by men, jasmine

Janhitā: one concerned with people's welfare

Jāni: daughter-in-law, an apsara

Jantumati: conceiver, earth

Janujā: born, a daughter

Jarita: Sage Mandapala's wife

Jārul: queen of flowers, myrtle flower

Jararāni: queen of fame

34

Jasrāh: narrator of the Hadith

Jaṭalikā: with twisted hair

Jaṭilā: complex, with twisted hair

Javitri: spice, mace

Jayā: victory, victorious, Parvati

Jayadevi: goddess of victory

Jayalakshmi: goddess of victory

Jayalalitā: as beautiful as victory, the goddess of victory

Jayamālā: garland of victory

Jayanā: bestower of victory

Jayanandini: daughter of victory, daughter of Lakshmi

Jayani: bringer of victory, daughter of Indra

Jayanti: finally victorious, a flag, daughter of Indra

Jayashree: goddess of victory

Jayitā : victorious

Jayitri : victorious

Jehān: beautiful flower

Jetashree: goddess of gains

Jhajharikā: a goddess

Jhālā: girl, heat of the sun

Jambāri: enemy of darkness, fire, Indra's thunderbolt, Indra

Jhankanā: desire

Jhankāriṅi: producing a tinkling sound, bell, anklet-worn woman, Durga, Ganga

Jharnā: flowing down, spring, streamlet, fountain

Jhaṭalik: lustre, splendour, light

Jhaṭi: shining, glittering, white jasmine

Jhillikā: sunshine, light, moth

Jhilmil: sparkling

Jhumari: ornament of the forehead

Jageeshā: desire to win

Jillian: girl

Jitavati: best among women, one who has won

Jityā: victorious

Jivanti: flower

Jivantikā: bestower of long life

Jivikā: source of life, water, occupation

Jogū: praising

Joshā: woman

Joshikā: cluster of buds, young woman

Joshyā: delightful

Joyce: just

Jugishā: one who wishes to be victorious

Jūhi: jasmine

Jūrni: glowing fires, blaze

Jutikā: camphor

Jwālā: flame, blaze, light, shine

Jwalana: flaming, shining

Jwālikā: blazing, lighted

Jyotā: the brilliant one

Jyoti: brilliant, like a flame, dawn, divine light, lightning, fire

Jyotinikā: with a shining face

Jyotirlekhā: a line of light

Jyotishmati: luminous, celestial, belonging to the world, brilliant, shining

Jyotsnā: moonlight, night, moonlit night, splendour, Durga

Jyotsni: moonlit night

Kāberi: full of water, courtesan

Kabilā: beloved

Kadali: banana tree

Kādambā: cloud, group, kadamba tree

Kādambari: emerging from the kadamba tree, female cuckoo, nectar from kadamba, flower, Saraswati

Kādambini: garland of clouds

Kadhapriyā: ever loved, ever friendly

Kadru: tawny, soma vessel, earth in a personified form

Kāhalā: mischievous, young woman, an apsara

Kāhini: mischievous, young

Kaileshwari: goddess of water, Durga

Kairavi: moonlight

Kairavini: water-born, white lotus plant

Kājal: collyrium, kohl

Kajri: collyrium-coloured, like a cloud

Kākali: cuckoo-voiced, a musical instrument

Kākalikā: with a sweet and low voice

Kākini: a small coin

Kakshi: of jungle, fragrant earth, perfume

Kakubhā: peak, splendour, beauty, wealth of flowers

Kakud: peak, symbol of royalty

Kalā: art, a small point, a part of the moon, an atom, still

Kālakanyā: daughter of tune

Kalāndikā: bestower of art and skills, wisdom, intelligence

Kalanishā: night of Diwali

Kalāpini: as blue as peacock's tail, night

Kalāvati: moonlight, well-versed in arts

Kalavinkā: cuckoo

Kaleshikā: black sandalwood

37

Kalee: destroyer of time, night

Kālika: dark blue, black, fragrant earth, fog, Durga

Kalika: bid, tender, fragrant, progressive

Kallolini: ever happy, surging stream

Kalpalatā: wish-giving creeper

Kalpanā: imagination, decoration

Kalpataru: wish-granting tree

Kalpavati: virtuous

Kalyā: eulogy, praise

Kalyānavati: propitious, beneficial, fortunate, excellent, Parvati

Kalyāni: auspicious, happy, beautiful

Kamā: beauty, radiance

Kāmadā: granting wishes

Kāmaduhā: granter of desires

Kāmadyū: granter of wishes

Kāmādhyā: granter of wishes, Durga

Kāmākshi: with beautiful and large eyes, Durga

Kamal: born of a lotus, beautiful, wealth, spring, desirous, Lakshmi

Kamalanayani: lotus-eyed

Kamaleekā: a small lotus

Kamalekshanā: lotus-eyed

Kamali: collection of lotuses, water, crane

Kamalini: lotus plant, collection of lotuses, fragrant, auspicious, beautiful, dear to the Gods

Kāmanā: desire

Kāmāyakā: desired abode

Kāmāyani: mirror of love

Kāmikā: desired

Kamilā: perfect one

Kāmini: desirable, loving, beautiful

Kāmitā: wished for, desired

Kāmrā: lovable, wish, desire

Kāmodi: that which excites

Kamrā: beautiful, attractive, loving

Kāmuka: desired

Kāmyā: desirable, beautiful, amiable

Kana: girl, eye

Kānaka: born of sand, Sita

Kanakalatā: golden vine

Kanakāmbarā: dressed in gold, golden, a flower

Kanakaprabhā: gold-lustred, golden bright

Kanakāvati: golden chain

Kanakavalli: golden creeper

Kanakavati: possessor of gold, golden

Kanakvi: a small kite

Kānan: forest, grove

Kānanalatā: forest maiden

Kanchanā: that which shines, wealth

Kānchanamālā: garland of gold

Kānchanaprabhā: as bright as gold

Kānchapi: connoisseur of glory, Saraswati's lute

Kānchi: shining, belled waistband

Kandarā: lute, hollow, cave

Kandharā: water bearer, cloud

Kanganā: bracelet

Kani: girl

Kaneech: creeper with blossoms

Kaneenā: youthful, pupil of the eye, little finger

Kanika: small, diminutive, girl

Kanishṭhā: little finger, youngest

Kanita: iris of the eye

Kanjari: bird, a musical instrument

Kankā: perfume of the lotus

Kakanā: bracelet, ornament, crest

Kankanika: small bell, tinkling ornament

Kankshā: desire, inclination

Kankshini: one who desires

Kannaki: devoted wife

Kannikā: maiden

Kāntā: beloved, perfume, earth

Kānti: beauty, glory, wish, decoration, a part of the moon

Kanyā: daughter, maiden

Kanyakā: maiden, the smallest, daughter

Kanyalā: girl

Kanyanā: maiden

Kanyāratnā: a gem of a girl

Kapālikā: Kali

Kapālini: Durga

Kapardikā: a small shell

Kapilā: daughter of Daksha

Kapishā: a river

Karavini: strong-armed, oleander flower

Karishmā: miracle

Karishni: goddess of wealth

Karkari: lute

Karidā: untouched, virginal

Karmishthā: very diligent

Karni: a good listener

Karnikā: creeper, heart of a lotus, earring

Karoli: Parvati

Kārpani: gladness

Karpūri: camphor-scented

Kārtiki: full-moon night, pious, holy

Karunā: compassion, tenderness

Karunesh: goddess

Karunyā: compassionate, praiseworthy, merciful

Kāshi: splendid, shining, sun

Kashmirā: a tree

Kastūri: musk-scented

Kasturikā: musk

Kāshvi: beautiful, shining

Kathleen: little darling

Kātyāyani: clad in red, Parvati

Kaukulikā: belonging to the universe

Kaumāri: virgin, Parvati

Kaushalikā: present, offering

Kausalyā: welfare, cleverness, skill

Kaushikā: drinking vessel, silk, cup

Kaushiki: covered, silken, Durga

Kautukā: giving pleasure, causing admiration, arousing curiosity

Kāvali: bangle

Kāveri: full of water, courtesan, turmeric

Kavikā: poetess

Kavitā: poem

Keeli: parrot

Keelin: slender, fair

Keerti: glory, fame, renown

Keertidā: bestower of fame

Keertimālini: garlanded with fame

Kelakā: sportive, one who knows the arts, artiste, playful

Kenāti: excelling all

Kesari: scented like saffron

Keshayantri: long-haired

Keshikā: long-haired

Keshini: long-haired, Durga

Ketaki: golden, a flower

Ketimati: gifted with brightness

Kevikā: a flower

Khalā: mischievous

Khalidā: immortal

Khaṇḍini: made of parts, earth

Kharikā: powered musk

Kharjuri: reaching the skies, date tree

Khashā: perfume, pervading the air

Kheli: moving in the sky, sun, bird, hymn, arrow

Khimyā: mercy

Khyāti: perception, celebrity, hymn of praise, idea, knowledge, glory, view, Lakshmi

Kiki: bhuejay (bird)

Kirsṭen: stone church

Kitāl: nectar, wine

Kim: chief

Kimnari: singer

Kimpunā: small and pious

Kimshuka: a tiny parrot

Kinjatā: brook

Kinkanā: small bell

Kiranmayi: full of rays

Kirmi: an image of gold

Kishori: maiden, adolescent

Kohā: cuckoo, date tree, Vishnu

Kokila: Indian cuckoo

Kolambi: Siva's lute

Komalā: soft, tender, delicate, beautiful

Koshin: bud, mango, Durga

Koyal: Indian cuckoo

Kraunchi: heron, snipe (bird)

Krinjalā: brook

Kriti: creation, action

Kriyā: action, performance, work

Kripā: compassion, kindness, favour

Krishnā: night, dark, pupil of the eye, a plant with dark blossoms, perfume, Durga

Krishnāngi: black-bodied, parrot

Krishnavalli: dark-leaved, basil

Krishnaveni: with dark blue braids

Krishni: dark night

Kritadyuti: with accomplished glory

Kritamālā: garland maker

Kritee: creation, accomplishment, enchantment

Krittikā: star-covered

Kritvi: accomplished

Krityā: replete with achievements, right, magical rites, proper

Krityahā: full of achievements

Kshamā: mercy, patience, of earth, the number one, Durga

Kshamāvati: with a merciful mind

Kshamāvati: one who is compassionate, enduring, forbearing

Kshamyā: earth

Kshavyā: of the earth

Kshanadā: bestower of moment or leisure, bestower of life, water, night

Kshānti: patience, endurance, indulgence

Kshapā: night

Kshatriyāni: wife of a noble warrior

Kshemā: welfare, security, tranquillity, bliss

Kshemagiri: mountain of security, full of security

Kshemakari: bestowing happiness and peace and security, Durga

Kshemyā: goddess of wealth, Durga

Kshiprā: fast

Kshirasāgarā: sea of milk

Kshirin: milky

Kshiti: abode, habitation, earth, soil of the earth, settlements, races of men

Kshitijā: born of the earth, Sita

Kshonā: immovable, earth

Kuhāritā: song of the cuckoo

Kuhū: cry of the cuckoo

Kujā: daughter of the earth, horizon, Sita, Durga

Kulānganā: highborn woman

Kulyā: virtuous, well born

Kumarādevi: goddess of children

Kumani: maiden, daughter, gold, jasmine, Durga, Sita

Kumārikā: girl, virgin, jasmine, Durga, Sita

Kumbhikā: a small water jar

Kumbhini: jar-shaped, earth

Kumkum: red, saffron, pollen

Kumud: lily, red, lotus

Kumudākshā: lotus-eyed, red-eyed

Kumudikā: bearer or wearer of water lilies

Kumudini: collection of white lilies

Kumālikā: cuckoo

Kundā: flower

Kundanikā: jasmine

Kundini: collection of jasmines

Kunjikā: belonging to the flower, nutmeg flower

Kunshi: shining

Kuntalā: perfume, lock of hair, plough

Kurangākshi: beautiful, doe-eyed

Kurangi: deer, spot in the moon

Kureerā: head ornament

Kusumā: like a flower, a blossom, yellow champaka flower

Kusumānjali: offering of flowers

Kusumitā: adorned with flower

Kuvalayiṅi: abounding in water lilies

Kuralayitā: adorned with water lilies

Labuki: lute

Laghupushpa: delicate flower

Lahari: wave

Lainey: sun ray

Lajja: modesty

Lajjana: modest

Lajjita: sky, coy, modest

Lajwanti: sensitive plant

Lajya: modesty

Lakini: one who takes and gives

Laksha: lac, plant

Lakshaki: dyed with lac, relating to lac

Lakshi: Lakshmi

Lakshita: beheld, distinguished

Lakshmi: fortune, prosperity, splendour, beauty, charm, success, pearl, goddess of fortune, turmeric

Lalantika: a long necklace

Lalatika: forehead ornament

Lalima: reddish glow, beautiful, charming, forehead ornament, symbol, banner

Lalita: woman, desirable, lovely, Durga, soft, gentle, graceful, voluptuous

Lalitaka: favourite daughter

Lalitangi: with a beautiful body

Lalitasya: grace, charm, beauty

Lalli: radiance, sweatness, blush, prestige

Laluka: necklace

Lambusha: a dangling ornament

Langapriya: adorable

Lapita: spoken, speech, voice

Lasha: saffron, turmeric

Lata: vine, slender woman, a string of pearls

Latabha: beautiful, handsome

Latamani: coral

Latika: forehead ornament, string of pearls, a small creeper

Lavalee: vine, custard apple

Lavaleekā: tiny vine

Lavaleenā: devoted, enraptured

Lavaña: lustrous, beautiful

Lavaneetā: extremely beautiful

Lavangi: of the clove plant

Lāvanyā: extremely beautiful

Lavañyamayi: full of beauty, full of charm

Lee: glade, poet, plum

Leelā: play, amusement, beauty, grace, pleasure, ease

Leelāvati: playful, beautiful, graceful, charming, Durga

Leenā: absorbed, merged, engrossed

Leigh: meadow

Leila: dark as night

Lekhā: line, streak, lightning, figure, mark, crescent moon, horizon, crest

Lenā: pearl

Lepākshi: with painted eyes

Leslie: dweller in grey castle

Liānā: creeper plant

Libby: consecrated to God

Libujā: vine

Lindsay: port, island

Linnet: bird

Lipikā: alphabet, writing, anointing, manuscript

Lochanā: eye, brightening, illuminating

Lohamukhitā: red pearl

Lohitā: red, ruby

Lohitākshi: red-eyed

Lohitamukti: ruby

Lohitāyani: red

Lohitikā: ruby

Lohityā: rice

Lokavyā: a deserver of heaven

Loksakshini: beholder of universe, goddess

Lolā: Lakshmi

Lolikā: a kind of sorrel

Lolini: woman

Lolitā: sorrows

Lonikā: beautiful woman

Lotikā: light reddish-brown

Loyanā: eye

Lucky: favoured by fortune

Luellā: elfin

Luni: Ganga

Lupitā: Sage Mandapala's wife

Madanlekhā: love letter, love sequence

Madanamanchūkā: aroused

Madanamajari: bird of love

Madani: vine, musk

Madanikā: excited, aroused

Madanayanti: exciting, jasmine, Durga

Madanyantikā: exciting, jasmine

Madayati: exciting, jasmine

Mādhavā: exotic, full of intoxication, exciting

Madhavashree: vernal beauty

Mādhavi: sweet, date flower, basil, intoxicating drink, Durga

Mādhavikā: collector of honey, creeper

Madhu: sweet, honey, soma, nectar, water, butter

Madhubālā: sweet maiden

Madhudhārā: stream of honey

Madhudivā: excited by honey, excited by spring, intoxicated

Madhujā: made of honey, honeycomb, earth

Madhukakshā: sweetness, dew

Madhūlikā: sweetness, bee, mustard

Madhumādhavi: a spring flower full of honey

Madhumati: rich in honey, spring-intoxicated, sweet, pleasant, agreeable

Madhumeetā: sweet friend

Madhupratikā: sweet-mouthed, with qualities of a yogini

Madhupushpā: spring flower, rain

Madhurākshi: with beautiful eyes

Mādhuri: sweetness, charm, wine, syrup, jasmine, a musical instrument

Madhurimā: sweetness, loveliness, charm

Madhushree: beauty of spring

Madhuvalini: gifted with nectar

Madhuwati: with a heady beauty

Madhuvidya: sweet knowledge

Madhwija: born of honey, an intoxicating drink

Madira: nectar, wine, intoxicating liquor

Madiravati: with intoxicating beauty

Madirekshana: with intoxicating eyes

Magha: gift, wealth, reward

Maghee: giving presents

Maghya: jasmine blossom

Maha: great, cow

Mahadyota: extremely shining

Mahajava: extremely fleet-footed

Mahajaya: extremely victorious

Mahalakshi: of the great sky

Mahallika: a female attendant

Mahanisha: greatest of the nights, Durga

Mahasadhvi: extremely chaste woman, Sita

Mahashree: great divinity, Lakshmi

Mahati: greatness, Narada's lute

Mahattavi: great star

Majayashas: very famous

Mahee: great world, earth

Mahela: woman, tenderness, marrow

Mahelika: woman

Maheshani: great lady, Parvati

Maheshi: Durga

Mahika: dew, frost

Mahima: greatness, glory, power, majesty, night, importance

Mahishada: master of the earth

Mahishaghni: slayer of the demon Mahish, Durga

Mahishee: queen, of high status, Ganga

Mahisuti: daughter of the earth, Sita

Mahita: flowing on the earth, greatness

Maheeti: Krishna's beloved Radha

Maheeya: exultation, happiness

Mahuli: enchanting voice

Maina: intelligence, starling (bird)

Maitrayani: friendly

Maitreyi: friendly

Maitri: friendship, generosity, goodwill

Maharandika: like nectar

Makee: heaven and earth conjoined

Makshika: bee

Mala: garland, rosary, necklace, row, line, wreath

Malada: bringer of fortune

Malasika: garlanded

Malashree: beautiful, garland

Malati: bud, blossom, virgin, moonlight, night, maid, jasmine

Malatika: made of jasmine

Malavati: garlanded, crowned

Malavi: princess of the Malavas

Malavika: of the Malavas

Malayavati: very fragrant

Malika: double jasmine, daughter, intoxicating drink, necklace

Malini: sweet smelling, jasmine, Durga, Ganga

Mallika: queen, garland, jasmine, daughter, necklace

Maluka: basil

Malyavati: garlanded

Mamata: motherly love, sense of ownership

Mamie: pearl

Manada: giving honour, a part of the moon

Manaka: according to the mind, loving woman, rosary, bead

Manani: indignant woman

Mananya: deserving praise

Manapreeti: dear to the heart, delight, pleasure

Manasā: born in the mind, heart, mental power, intention

Manashree: wealth of mind

Mānasi: spiritual adoration

Manasitā: wisdom

Manastokā: mental satisfaction, Durga

Mānasvi: controller of mind, intelligence

Mānasvini: controller of mind, proud, virtuous, high-minded, noble, Durga

Manavarā: pleasing to the mind

Mānavi: wife of Manu, goddess of learning

Mānavikā: young girl

Manāyi: Manu's wife

Mandākini: Milky Way, slow mover

Mandanā: gay, cheerful

Mandarā: slow, firm, large

Mandarāvati: bearer of coral flowers

Mandarikā: coral tree

Māndavi: able administrator

Māndhāri: bearer of honour

Mandirā: of temple, sacred, melodious, slow sound, venerated

Mandrā: pleasant, low-voiced, charming, agreeable

Maneeshā: reflection, thought, wisdom, idea, intelligence, request, wish, hymn, prayer, consideration

Mangalā: auspicious, fortunate, faithful wife, jasmine, Durga, Parvati

Mangalee: auspicious, scented with jasmine

Mangalyā: auspicious, sandalwood, wood apple, Durga

Mani: jewel

Manibhūmi: a mine of pearls

Manidhārini: bejewelled, ornamented

Manijatā: with crystal-clear water

51

Manika: of jewels

Manikarnika: jewelled earring

Manikuttika: inlaid with jewels

Manimala: necklace of jewels, lustrous, beautiful, Lakshmi

Manimanjari: cluster of jewels

Maninga: treasure of jewels

Manini: determined, self-respecting

Maniprabha: jewels, splendour

Maniratna: jewel

Manishi: longing

Manishika: intelligence, understanding

Manishka: wisdom, intelligence

Manisraj: a garland of jewels

Manishthaka: little finger

Maneeya: glass bead

Manja: cluster of blossoms

Manjari: cluster of flowers, spring, flower

stem, bud, sprout, sprig, vine, pearl, flower

Manjarika: small cluster of flowers, small pearl, basil plant

Manjee: cluster of flowers

Manjeeta: winner of heart

Manjiman: bearer of flowers, elegance, beauty

Manjira: anklet

Manju: attracting the heart, charming, sweet, beautiful, lovely, pleasant

Manjula: captivating the heart, lovely, beautiful, charming, pleasing, arbour, spring, bower

Manjulata: vine of beauty

Manjulika: beautiful

Manjumati: with a lovely heart, compassionate, humane looking

Manjunashi: connoisseur of beauty, a pretty woman, Durga

Manjushree: divine, beauty, Lakshmi

Manjutara: most lovely

Manodari: pleasing to the heart

Manohara: winning the heart, stealer of heart, yellow jasmine

Manohari: stealer of heart

Manorama: pleasing the mind, beautiful, charming, musk jasmine

Manorita: of the mind, desire, wish

Manotee: daughter in mind, vow of offering to a diety

Manovati: desired by the mind

Manovinda: amusing to the mind

Mantika: thoughtful

Mantramala: garland of hymns, collection of prayers and chants

Mantrana: advice, counsel, deliberation

Mantrini: the queen of chess

Manu: of the mind, desirable

Manuja: woman

Manushi: woman, humane

Manya: worthy of honour and respect

Manyanti: honourable

Manuavati: esteemed, honoured

Maralee: female swan

Maralika: small swan

Mardava: kindness, gentleness

Mareechika: mirage

Mareesha: respectable, worthy

Marina: soft woollen cloth

Marjani: purifying, cleansing

Martha: lady

Marula: rock-born, born with Shiva's blessings

Marya: boundary, mark, limit

Masar: sapphire, emerald

Mashi: dark-complexioned

Masma: fair-complexioned

Matali: mother's friend

Matallika: anything excellent of its kind

Matana: gift

Mātangi: roaming carefree, cloud, Durga

Mātangini: roaming at will

Mati: prayer, intelligence, devotion, intention, hymn, memory, opinion, motion, wish

Mātrika: divine mother

Maurvikā: low string

Māyā: illusion, wealth, art, wisdom, compassion, Durga

Mayūrānki: with peacock marks, a jewel

Mayūri: peahen

Mayurikā: with peacock feathers

Medhā: wisdom, intelligence, tact

Medhani: of intelligence, Brahma's wife

Medhāvikriti: with the fame of wisdom

Medhyā: vigorous, fresh, wise, intelligent, full of sap, strong, clean, pure

Medini: fertile, earth

Meenā: goblet of wine, a gem, fish, multi-coloured glass, stick

Meenākshi: fish-eyed, Parvati

Meenāli: fish catcher, fisherwoman

Meenāti: like fish, voluptuous

Meerā: ocean, sea, boundary, limit

Meetā: tried and tested, measured and gauged, friend

Meeti: friend

Megha: cloud, mass

Meghadeepā: light of the cloud, lightning

Meghajā: born of the clouds, water, large pearl

Meghamala: garland of clouds

Meghamanjari: cloud, blossom

Meghana: rumbling of clouds, thunder

Meghanāda: with the sound of clouds, thunder

Megharangikā: cloud-coloured, dark-complexioned

Megharanjini: delighter of clouds

54

Megharekha: row of clouds

Meghashvana: sounding like clouds, sounding like thunder

Meghavahini: riding on a cloud

Meghavalee: row of clouds

Meghayanti: creator of clouds, creator of cloudy weather

Mehala: knower of the self, girdle

Meher: kindness, compassion

Mehtab: moonlight

Mekhala: belt, mountain slope, river Narmada

Melvina: hand-maiden

Mena: intellect, woman, speech, celestial nymph

Menaja: Parvati

Menaka: born of the mind, Parvati

Menavati: possessing intellect, Parvati

Menita: intelligent, wise

Mercy: compassionate

Meruprabha: of great splendour

Merushree: the most beautiful

Madhushi: bountiful, generous

Mihika: mist, snow

Milika: desiring union

Minali: fisherwoman

Minati: entreaty, request

Minnie: remembrance, love

Minoti: vow, assurance

Mishi: sugarcane, dill

Mitali: friendship

Mitra: companion, friend, associate

Mitravinda: having companions

Mitushi: with limited desires

Modaki: pleasing, delighting

Modayantika: delighting, rejoicing, jasmine

Modini: musk

Mohana: beautiful, infatuating, alluring

Mohani: charming, infatuating

Mohini: fascinating, jasmine

Moirā: great, better

Mokshā: redemption

Monā: alone

Moongā: coral

Morgance: sea-dweller

Morikā: peahen

Morni: peahen

Moti: pearl

Mridini: good earth, soil

Mridu: gentle, soft, tender, mild, delicate, a vine of red grapes

Mridukā: tender, soft

Mridulā: tender, mild, soft

Mridvikā: gentleness, softness, mildness, bunch of red grapes, vine

Mrigākshi: deer-eyed

Mrigalochanā: doe-eyed

Mriganayanā: fawn-eyed

Mrigangnā: doe

Mrigekshanā: doe-eyed

Mrigi: doe, deer's mother

Mrigishnā: doe-eyed

Mrikshni: rain cloud, torrent

Mrināli: lotus root

Mrinālikā: lotus root

Mrinālini: collection of lotuses, sacred, tender, fragrant, venerated, dear to the gods

Mringangi: delicate, soft-bodied

Mrishanā: reflection, thought, deliberation

Mritsā: fragrant soil, good earth

Mritsnā: good earth, fertile and excellent soil

Mrittikā: earth, clay, loam

Mudā: happiness, joy, delight

Muditā: happy, joyous, pleased

Mudi: happy, moonshine

Muditapushpā: happy flower, blooming flower

Mudrā: sign, seal, posture, signatory

Mudulā: soft, sweet

Mughdā: beautiful, innocent, young, guileless, gentle, tender

Mughākshi: fair-eyed

Mugdhavadhū: young, lovely

Mukhashri: with a beautiful face

Muktā: pearls

Muktabhā: with a pearly sheen, double jasmine

Muktālatā: string of pearls

Muktāli: pearl necklace

Muktāmbari: clad in clothes of pearl

Mukti: freedom, liberation

Muktikā: pearl

Mukulikā: small blossom

Mukundā: precious stone, gem, liberator

Mukuṭā: wearing a crown

Mundali: Durga

Mundari: ring

Muniā: small girl

Muralee: flute, melodious, sweet, enchanting, harmonious

Muralikā: small flute

Muralini: lotus

Nabhanyā: emerging from heaven, celestial, heavenly, ethereal

Nabhasarit: river of the sky, Milky Way

Nabhasindhu: Milky Way, celestial Ganga

Nabhashwāti: born of the sky, lightning, thunder

Nabhaswati: bearer of the sky, young, wind

Naḍantikā: destruction of reed

Nadeemā: friend

Nāganandini: mountain-born

Nāganikā: serpent maiden

Nāgapushpikā: flower of the mountains, yellow jasmine

Nāgashri: wealth of the serpents

Nāgavithi: row of serpents, path of the moon

Nageezā: precious thing

Nāgendri: mountain lord's daughter, serpent lord's daughter, elephant kings daughter, emerging through the Himalayas

Naginā: mountain-obtained, gem, jewel

Naidhruvā: almost perfect, nearing eternity, Parvati

Naimā: belonging to one, striving for the absolute

Naimalochani: with twinkling eyes

Nainikā: pupil of the eye

Nākanāri: celestial woman

Nākavanitā: heavenly woman

Nakshatramālā: garland of stars, necklace of 27 pearls

Naktā: night

Naktamukhā: evening

Nakti: night

Naladā: nectar of a flower

Nālakini: lotuses in abundance

Nalami: fragrant nectar, Shiva's lute

Nalikā: perfume

Nalini: lotus, water lily, abundances of lotuses, fragrant, beautiful, sacred, dear to the gods

Nalininandanā: lotus bud

Namitā: humble, lowed, modest, worshipper, submissive, devotee

Namratā: humbleness, modesty, meekness, submissiveness

Namyā: venerable, to be bowed to, night

Nandā: happiness, prosperity, delight, Durga

Nandanā: daughter, delighting, Durga

Nandanamālā: garland of delight

Nandanti: daughter, delighting

Nandayanti: bestowing joy

Nandi: joy, happiness, Durga

Nandikā: pleasure-giving

Nandini: delightful, daughter, Durga

Nanditā: pleasure

Nārā: near, joyous

Nārāyani: belonging to Narayana, Vishnu's wife, Durga, Lakshmi, Ganga

Nardishā: ocean

Nargis: narcissus flower

Nāristhā: dear to a woman

Narmadā: pleasure-giver

Narmadyuti: happy, merry, bright with joy

Nartaki: dancer

Natā: curved, arced

Nati: modesty, humanity

Nautan: new, fresh

Navaditā: pleased, happy

Navamallikā: new creeper, jasmine

Navāngi: with a fresh body, exquisite woman, refreshing woman

Navikā: new, fresh, young

Naveenā: new, young, fresh

Navishṭhi: hymn, song of praise

Naveeyā: new, young

Navya: new

Nayajā: daughter of wisdom

Nayanā: of eye, pupil of the eye

Nayanapreeti: delighting the eye

Nayantārā: star of one's eye, beloved, very dear to one

Nāzimā: song

Nāzirā: equal

Nāzini: beautiful woman

Nedā: born on Sunday

Neechitā: full of, flowing down, covered, Ganga

Neetā: blue, indigo plant

Neelakshā: blue-eyed

Neelam: moon, cloud, sapphire

Neelamani: blue gem, sapphire

Neelaneeraj: blue water lily

Neelānjanā: lightning, antimony (blue metal)

Neelānjasā: blue-lined lightning

Neelapadmā: blue lotus

Neeli: indigo, antimony

Neelimā: blue

Neelini: indigo plant

Neenā: slender, ornamented

Neerā: water-laden, juice, liquor

Neerajā: water-born, water lily, pearl

Neerajākshi: lotus-eyed, beautiful

Neerajitā: illuminated

Neeru: only, complete

Neetā: led, guide, modest, correct, well-behaved

Neetikā: guide, leader, ethical

Nehā: loving, affectionate

Netravati: observant, wise, Lakshmi

Nibhā: resembling, similar

Nichikā: consisting of parts, constituting a whole, perfect

Nichitā: fully covered, Ganga

Niddhā: possessing treasure, resolute, giving, attempting

Niddi: supreme God

Nidhyāti: reflection, meditation

Nidhi: to shine upon, to bestow

Nihārika: misty, Milky Way

Nikhar: beauty, lustre, brightness

Nileema: brightness, bluishness

Nilofer: blue lotus, lily

Nimā: to measure, to adjust

Nimishā: twinkling of an eye

Nimlochā: sunset

Nimmesh: twinkling of the eye

Nimmi: unattached

Nimrukti: sunset

Ninu: to accomplish, to offer as sacrifice

Nipā: to guard

Nirajākshi: lotus-eyed, beautiful

Nirājitā: enlightened

Niranjanā: spotless, pure, full-moon day, Durga

Nirbhā: shining forth, progress, appearance

Nirbhāshitā: illumined

Niriksha: not seen before, expectation, hope, unseen

Nirjari: ever young, fresh, immortal, ambrosia

Nirlep: pure, sinless

Nirmārshti: washing, ablution

Nirmitā: constructed

Nirūpā: formless like God

Nirupāmā: peerless, unequalled

Nirvā: refreshing, blowing like wind, exhilarating

Nirvani: goddess of bliss

Nishā: night, dream, vision

Nishādi: twilight

Nishājal: water of the night, dew

Nishama: matchless

Nishāpushpā: night flower, white water lily

Nishchalā: fixed, immovable, earth

Nischirā: emerging, appearing

Nishi: exciting, strengthening

Nisidh: gift, offering

Nishita: night

Nishkā: pure, honest, golden vessel, golden ornament for neck

Nishkuṭikā: pleasure grove near house

Nishnā: clever, skilful

Nishṭhā: determination, firmness, devotion, faith, loyalty, fidelity

Nitambini: beautiful woman

Nityā: eternal, constant, indispensable

Nityashri: ever beautiful

Nityasundari: eternally beautiful

Nivedita: offered to God

Nivedna: entreaty, plea

Niyati: fate, restraint, destiny, religious duty, Durga

Nolā: famous, noble

Noyā: beautifully ornamented

Nukri: bird

Nūpur: ankle and toe ornaments, anklet

Nūtan: young, new, fresh, strange, curious

Nuti: praise, worship, reverence

Nyāyikā: logician

Nyjā: natural

Octaviā: eight born

Odati: refreshing, dawn

Ojalā: shining, radiant, lustre

Ojasvitā: splendour, lustre, brilliance

Ojaswini: bright, shining, powerful, vigorous, brave, energetic

Olympiā: heavenly

Omalā: bestower of the sacred syllable Om, bestower of birth-life-death, earth

Omā: Parvati

Omeeshā: goddess of the sacred syllable, goddess of birth-life-death

Omkārā: syllable Om, auspicious beginning

Omvati: possessor of Om power, sacred

Ondaryā: broadminded, bountiful

Onile: River Nile

Oormi: wave, musical term

Oristā: a tree

Orvanā: fairy's name

Osha: early morning

Oshadi: medicine, herb, healing power, possessor of light

Oshmā: summer

Ottarā: Abhimanyu's wife

Padmā: lotus, coloured one, Lakshmi

Padmabālā: daughter of the lotus

Padmajā: born of a lotus, Lakshmi

Padmakarā: with lotus in hand

Padmalānchanā: surrounded by lotuses, Lakshmi, Saraswati

Padmālayā: dwelling in a lotus, Lakshmi

Padmamālini: lotus-garlanded, Lakshmi

Padmanayi: made of lotus flowers

Padmanā: lotus-faced, Lakshmi, Saraswati

Padmānjali: offering of lotuses

Padmaprabhā: with the light of the lotus, lotus-coloured

Padmapriyā: lover of lotuses

Padmarati: lover of lotuses

Padmarūpa: with the beauty of a lotus, Lakshmi

Padmasushā: dwelling in the lotus, Ganga, Lakshmi, Durga

Padmashree: divine lotus, as beautiful as a lotus

Padmāvati: full of lotus flowers, Lakshmi

Padmini: lotus, collection of lotuses

Padminikā: multitude of lotuses

Pāhaḍi: hillock

Paijini: tinkling anklets

Pajaswati: steady, strong, brilliant, firm

Pākeezā: pure, clean

Pakshālikā: full of feathers

Pakshiñi: full-moon day, female bird

Palakshi: white

Palāshini: foliage-covered

Pālitā: protected, cherished

Pallavi: young shoot, sprouting

Pallavikā: like a blossom, scarf

Palmā: palm-bearing, pilgrim

Pamelā: all honey

Panchajanā: bearer of five sons

Panchajani: made of five elements

Pānchāli: companion of five, doll

Pānchālikā: doll

Paṇḍā: wisdom, knowledge, learning

Pāndarā: white, pale

Pāndurā: yellow-clad lady

Paṇihatā: created by hand

Panishṭhi: admiration, praise

Pānjari: impression of full hand

Pankajākshi: lotus-eyed

Pankajini: full of lotuses

Pannā: emerald

Panu: admiration

Panyā: admired, excellent, glorious, astonishing, praiseworthy

Paramā: that, which is transcendent, perfect woman

Paramānganā: supreme woman, beautiful woman

Paramātmikā: the highest, supreme, the greatest, possessing a soul

Parapushiṭā: female cuckoo

Pari: fairy, beautiful woman

Paridhi: sun's halo, moon's halo, lamp

Pārijāt: born, coral, jasmine

Pariksha: test, trial

Parimugdha: extremely lovely, bewitchingly lovely

Parineetā: led around, total, complete, married woman

Parinishṭha: living at the top, higher point, full knowledge, full accomplishment

Parishobhitā: adorned, beautiful

Parisraj: garland

Pariveeta: extremely liked, totally free

Paramāganā: excellent woman

Parnashā: feeding on leaves

Parnini: plumed, winged, leafy

Parokshi: beyond perception, mysterious, not discernible

Pārthivi: daughter of the earth, Sita, Lakshmi

Pāru: fire, sun

Pārul: beautiful, gracious, practical

Parvāka: purifier, whirlwind, storm

Parvani: full-moon day

Pārvati: of the mountains, mountain stream

Parveen: competent

Parvini: festival

Pashminā: soft and fine wood

Pastyā: house, household goddess

Pāṭalee: trumpet flower

Patangana: butterfly

Patangi: flying

Patangika: small bird, small bee

Paṭeshwari: goddess of clothes, Durga

Pāthamanjari: decorating the path, maker of easy path

Pāthojini: collection of lotus plants

Pathyā: of path, way

Pātri: vessel, competent, worthy, protector, Durga

Pattradini: main queen of the king

Pattralekhā: decorated with lines of fragrant spices

Pattrapushpā: made of leaves and flowers, basil

Paṭumati: with a clever mind

Pauralikā: pleasant to citizens

Paushṭi: strong, satisfied, voluptuous

Pāvakā: purifier, storm

Pāvakārchis: a flash of fire

Pāvaki: purifying, Saraswati

Pavani: pure, holy, purifying, basil, Ganga

Pavitrā: pure, holy, sacred, beneficent, basil

Payal: of the foot, anklet, strength

Payasvāni: a river

Payoshi: milky

Pearl: precious gem

Pelavā: delicate, fine, tender

Peelā: halting

Peelak: yellow, golden-coloured

Peelu: blossom, flower

Peetadiptā: yellow light, of yellow colour

Peetayuthi: collection of yellow, yellow jasmine

Peetikā: saffron, yellow jasmine, honey, turmeric

Persis: Persian woman

Peshani: beautiful, well-formed

Phalyā: flower, bud

Phullāmbikā: woman, a bloom, woman in full bloom

Phullarā: graceful woman

Pikee: cuckoo

Pinākini: bow-shaped, with the low

Pingākshi: tawny-eyed

Pingalā: Lakshmi

Pinjalā: confused

Pippin: beautiful girl

Pixie: elf

Polikā: opal

Poonam: full-moon day

Potri: purifier, Durga

Pratha: light, radiance, splendour

Prabhāta: goddess of dawn

Prabhāti: song of the morning

Prabhāvali: shining, graceful, radiant

Prabhāvati: radiant, luminous, splendid, quick-witted, intelligent, bright

Prabhūti: arisen, welfare, success, wealth, well-being

Prachandikā: very fiery, Durga

Prachāyikā: gatherer of flowers

Prāchikā: driving, female falcon

Prachodikā: inflamer

Prādha: very distinguished, supreme, eminent

Pradhāna: chief, source, original, intellect, understanding, most important

Pradhi: disc of the moon

Pradeepikā: illuminator, torch, a small lamp

Pradeepti: radiance, light, lustre

Prafulla: blossomed, greatly delighted

Pragati: progress

Prahasanti: smiling, laughing, jasmine

Prajaktā: mother of people, goddess of creation

Prajāshikā: enlightener, illuminator, bright, stunning, brilliant, celebrated, renowned

Prajnyā: goddess

Prajwala: lighted

Prakāshini: lighting up, making visible

Prakhyā: appearance, brightness, splendour, renown, celebrity

Prakirti: highly celebrated, renowned, celebration, declaration

Prakriti: nature, original, primary substance

Prakyā: shining, celebrity

Pramā: foundation, knowledge

Pramadā: joyous, enchanting, intoxicating, woman, handsome

Pramandani: with a swan's gait

Pramikā: highest, best, greatest

Pramila: enervation

Pramiti: wisdom, right perception, prudence

Pramod: great happiness

Pramodini: delight

Prānati: salutation, reverence, obeisance

Prānavati: full of life, powerful, strong

68

Pranayini: devotee, worshipper, beloved

Pranayita: animated, lively

Praneeta: led, advanced, conducted, promoted, executed, finished, established, composed, produced, performed, holy water

Praneeti: leading, guidance, conduct

Pranjali: upright, honest, sincere

Prapti: achievement, arrival, discovery, occurrence, obtainment

Prarthana: prayer

Prasha: powerful, forceful

Prashami: tranquil, calm

Prasanna: pleasing, propitiating

Prashasta: happy, praised, clear, calm, consecrated

Prashasti: praise, fame, glory

Prasatti: satisfaction, purity, clearness, brightness

Prasiddhi: fame, success, attainment, achievement

Prashuchi: extremely pure

Prasuti: emerging, appearance, offspring, child

Prata: dawn

Pratapi: brilliant, glorious, powerful, majestic

Prateechya: with foresight

Prateeka: symbolic, beautiful, image

Pratibha: image, splendour, light, idea, wit, intelligence, understanding, appearance

Pratigna: vow, promise

Pratima: image, resemblance, symbol, idol

Pratishruti: answer, assent, promise

Pratishtha: stability, steadfastness, base, celebrity, fame, foundation, pre-eminence, support

Prava: blowing forth

Pravara: best among women

Pravirtā: wisdom

Preeti: joy, satisfaction, pleasure, love

Prekshā: seeing, beholding, viewing

Premā: love, beloved, kindness, affection

Premlatā: vine of love

Premāvati: full of love

Preranā: direction, command, inspiration

Preritā: one who is encouraged

Preshthā: dearest, most beloved

Pretashini: Kali

Prishani: tender, gentle

Prishni: earth, cloud, milk, ray of light, starry sky

Prishti: ray of light, touch

Prithikā: jasmine

Prethukeerti: one whose fame has reached far

Prithvi: earth

Pritibālā: affectionate girl

Priyā: beloved, dear, jasmine

Priyadarshikā: good-looking

Priyadarshini: dear to the sight

Priyadattā: bestowed with love, earth

Priyālā: bestowing pleasure, bunch of grapes, vine, butter tree

Promilā: primrose, flower

Pūjā: worship, adoration, honour, respect, reverence, veneration

Pūjitā: honoured, goddest, adored, worshipped

Pulomā: to the thrilled

Pundarikā: like a lotus

Puneetā: holy, pious, sacred

Punyajani: meritorious

Punyashlokā: well spoken of, Sita, Draupadi

Punyavati: full of virtues, blessed, beautiful, fortunate, honest, happy, righteous

Puralā: protector of fortresses, Durga

Purandhi: woman, generosity, liberality

Pūrani: completing, fulfilling, satisfying, Durga

Puranjani: intelligence, understanding

Purāvati: going ahead, proceeding

Puravi: living, inviting

Pūrnā: complete, abundant, content, part of the moon

Pūrnimā: full-moon night or day

Pūrnodarā: with satiated appetite

Purukripā: full of mercy, compassionate

Purupriyā: dear to many

Purūvi: fulfiller, satiater

Pūshā: nourishing, cherishing

Pūshanā: protector, nourishes

Puskharā: like a lotus

Pushkarini: lotus pond

Pushpā: like a flower, blossom, flower

Pushpajā: born of a flower, nectar

Pushpamanjari: flower blossom, blue lotus

Pushpāngi: flower-bodied

Pushparenu: pollen, dust of flowers

Pushpavalli: flower vine

Pushpaveni: garland of flowers

Pushpendū: moon of flowers, white lotus

Pushpi: like a flower, beautiful, flower, fragrant, blossom, soft, tender

Pūtā: purified, clear, bright

Pūti: purity

Putli: pupil of the eye

Putrikā: daughter, doll, puppet, small idol

Pyāri: beloved, dear

Qabalā: responsibility
Qabilā: consenting
Qabool: accepted

Qadirā: powerful
Qailā: one who speaks
Qamrā: moon
Qaniāh: contented
Qilarā: fragrant
Qubilā: agreeable

Rachnā: creation, accomplishment, production

Raḍellā: elfin, advisor

Rādhā: full-moon day, lightning, prosperity, success

Rādhanā: speech

Rādhani: worship

Radhikā: prosperous, successful, Radha

Rāgā: beauty, melody, feeling, harmony, passionate

Rāgalatā: passion creeper

Rāgamayā: full of passion, red, full of colour, full of love, dear, beloved

Rāgavati: full of love, beloved, coloured

Rāginī: melody, love, attachment, Lakshmi

Rahni: love, affection

Rāhuratnā: jewel of Rahu, hyacinth

Rainā: night

Rajalakshmi: royal dignity

Rāji: night

Rajini: night

Rajyavati: princess, possessing a kingdom

Rākānishā: full-moon night

Rākiñi: night

Rakshā: protection, a charm or amulet for protection

Rakshāmani: jewel of protection

Rakshanā: protecting, safeguarding

Rakshi: wife of Sun god, queen

Rakshitā: protected

Raktā: red, painted, beloved, pleasant, dear

Raktahansā: red swan, happy soul

Raktakanchan: red gold

Raktakumud: red lotus

Raktapadmā: red lotus

Raktapallavā: red leaf, with red leaves

Raktapushpā: red-flowered, pomegranate blossom

Ramā: beautiful, charming, enchanting, fortune, opulence, red earth, splendour, vermilion

Ramādevi: goddess of beauty, lovely woman

Rāmakeli: sport of Lakshmi

Rāmakiri: of omnipresent nature, all-pervading

Ramakrit: causing rest

Rāmalā: lover, bestower of pleasure

Ramanā: enchanting, worthy of being loved, beloved, charming

Ramaneetā: elegance, beauty

Ramañi: beautiful, charming, delighting, joy, loving, pleasure, sexual union

Ramanikā: worth loving, attractive, pleasing

Ramatārā: star of fortune, basil plant

Rāmāyani: mirror of Rama, one well versed in the *Ramayana*

Rambhā: agreeable, lovable, pleasing, staff, plantain

Rāmita: bestower of pleasure, lover

Ramyā: enchanting, enjoyable

Ramyarūpā: with a lovely form

Ramyashree: most desired

Ranadā: making a sound, bestower of battles

Ranhitā: efficient, quick

Ranjitā: victorious in battle

Ranlakshmi: goddess of war, fortunes of war

Rangabhūti: born of love, full-moon night

Rangajā: born of love, vermilion

Rangamānikyā: beloved to Krishna

Rangati: coloured, agreeable, excited, lovable, passionate

Rangitā: charmed, coloured, delighted, painted

Ranhitā: quick, swift

Ranjanā: charming, exciting, pleasing, perfume, saffron, turmeric

Ranjikā: pleaser, charming, pleasing, exciting, love, red sandalwood

Ranjini: amusing, charming, colouring, delighting, entertaining, pleasing

Ranjitā: coloured, delighted, made happy, pleased

Rāno: peacock's tail

Ranvā: agreeable, delightful, gay, joyous, pleasant

Ranvitā: gay, joyous

Ranyā: pleasant

Rasā: essence, grapes, juice, love, charm, delight, nectar, passion, quicksilver, sentiment

Rāsā: full of essence, full of sentiments, play, noise, sport

Rasanā: knower of taste, taste, perception

Rasanikā: full of feeling, impassioned

Rasapriyā: fond of juice

Rasavanti: charming, delighting, emotional, sentimental

Rashanā: cord, rope, ray of light, perfume

Rashikā: elegant, full of passion, aesthetic, with discrimination, tasteful, sentimental

Rashmi: sunbeam, moonbeam, ray, rope

Rashmikā: tiny ray of light

Rasikā: aesthetic, elegant, gracious

Raswanti: affection

Rasyā: with essence, emotional, full of feelings, juicy, sentimental

Rathachitrā: like a multicoloured chariot

Rathantarā: one who sits inside the chariot

Rathāntari: dweller of the chariot

Rathyā: crossword, highway, group of chariots

Rati: love, desire, pleasure, passion, enjoyment, part of the moon

Rathihara: causing pleasure

Ratija: daughter of truth

Ratimada: intoxicated with love

Ratipreeti: love, pleasure, passion, conjoined

Ratna: jewel

Ratnakala: piece of jewel

Ratnamala: jewelled necklace

Ratnamalavati: with a necklace of jewels

Ratnamanjari: jewel, blossom

Ratnambari: clad in jewels

Ratnangi: with jewelled limbs

Ratnaprabha: the shine of jewels, earth

Ratnarashi: collection of jewels, sea

Ratnarekha: line of jewels, ornamented, very precious, very gracious, embellished

Ratnasu: producing jewels, earth

Ratnavali: necklace of jewels

Ratnavar: best among precious things, gold

Ratnavati: full of jewels, earth

Ratnolka: jewelled meteor

Ratnottama: best jewel

Ratri: might

Ratridevi: goddess of the night, white lotus opening at night, moon

Ratrika: night

Ratu: truthful, true, speech, Ganga

Ratiya: daughter of truth

Raupya: silvery, made of silver

Ravichandrika: glory of sun, moonlight

Ravija: born of the sun

Ravipriya: beloved of the sun

Ravishta: beloved of the sun, orange tree

Rebha: singer of praise

Rediatā: goddess

Reenā: melted, dissolved

Reeti: auspiciousness, course, motion, prosperity, remembrance, protection, streak, stream

Reetikā: of stream, brass

Rejākshi: fiery eyes

Rekhā: line, streak

Reṉukā: born of dust

Reṉumati: pollen-laden

Reshmā: silken

Reshman: silky, soothing

Revā: mover, agile, quick, swift

Revati: wealth, prosperity

Rhonḍā: good spear

Ribhyā: worshipped

Richā: praise, hymn, splendour, collection of *Vedas*

Richelle: powerful ruler, brave one

Riddhi: abundance, prosperity, success, wealth, supremacy, supernatural power, Lakshmi, Parvati

Riddhimā: prosperous, successful

Ridū: charming, pleasant, soft

Rihānā: sweet basil

Rijuvani: giving liberally, earth

Rikshā: the best, star, female bear

Rikshambikā: mother of the stars, mother of bears

Rishikā: female sage

Rishṭā: sword, mother of apsaras

Ritā: season

Riyā: singer

Roberṭā: bright, famous

Rochamānā:consisting of light, agreeable, bright, shining, splendid

Rochnā: brightness, light, beautiful, handsome, woman, bright sky, red, lotus

Rochani: delightful, agreeable

Rochi: beam, light, ray

Rochiras: aura, glow, light

Rochukā: causing pleasure, pleaser, delighter

Rodasi: heaven and earth conjoined, earth

Rohanti: climbing, vine

Rohee: rising up, red, doe

Rohini: ascending, increasing, tall, mother of cows, red cow, sandalwood tree

Rohitā: red, daughter of Brahma

Romā: full of hair

Romashā: with thick hair

Romolā: charming, thick-haired

Ropanā: causing to grow, healing

Roshansā: desire, wish

Roshini: eyesight, light

Rowenā: red-haired, rugged

Royimā: ascending, growing

Rishmā: moonbeam

Rishvā: high, great, noble, elevated

Ritu: fixed time, period, season, order

Ritumbharā: of divine truth, filled with season, earth

Ritushree: queen of the seasons, splendour of the seasons

Ritusthalā: abode of light, abode of seasons

Ruby: precious stone

Ruchā: brightness, desire, light, splendour, voice of the mynah

Ruchi: taste, beauty, desire, light, lustre, pleasure

Ruchikā: of taste, desirable, shining, ornament

Ruchirā: charming, dainty, desirable, pleasing, dainty

Ruchitā: sweet, bright, dainty, desirable, radiant, pleasing, lover

Rūdhi: birth, ascent, fame, rise

Rudrāni: Parvati

Rudrapushpa: red blossom, China rose

Rudrasi: red, like Rudra

Ruhā: risen, mounted, grown

Ruhāni: spiritual, of higher values

Rūhi: ascending, of higher value, soul

Ruhikā: riser, longing, desire

Rukmarekhā: golden line

Rukmavati: possessing gold, as beautiful as gold, golden

Rukmiṇi: mother of Pradyumna, an incarnation of Lakshmi, queen of Krishna

Rumā: salty, salt mine, ornament

Rūpā: bearer of former silver, earth

Rūpāli: beautiful, excellent in form

Rūpāngi: with a beautiful body

Rūpashree: divinely beautiful

Rūpasi: beautiful

Rūplekhā: appearance

Rūpmaṇi: beautiful maiden

Rūpmati: possessing beauty

Rūpshikā: crest of beauty, very beautiful

Rūpvati: possessed with beauty, handsome

Rūpavidyā: form of knowledge

Rūpeshwari: goddess of beauty

Rūpikā: having a form and figure, shape, appearance, gold coin, silver coin

Rūpiṇikā: having a beautiful form, corporeal, embodied

Rupwanti: beautiful girl

Rushmā: calm, angerless

Rūsaṇā: adorning, covering, decoration

Rushati: white, fair in complexion

Rutikā: ascender, wish

S

Sabine: sublime woman

Sabira: patient

Sabita: politeness, decency, civilised, good manners

Sabra: to rest

Sabrina: a goddess

Sacheeta: attentive, thoughtful

Sachu: happiness, pleasure

Sadajyoti: eternal lamp

Sadakanta: always loved

Sadasheesh: good blessing

Sadashiva: ever belonging to Shiva, ever kind and happy, Durga

Sadhaka: efficient, effective, magical, productive, Durga

Sadhana: accomplishment, adorations, means, performance, worship

Sadhika: accomplished, efficient, skilful, worshipper, Durga

Sadhri: conqueror

Sadhvi: chaste, faithful, honest, noble, pious, peaceful, virtuous, unerring

Sadhya: perfection, accomplishment

Sadvati: pious, righteous, truthful

Safa: clarity, purity of mind

Sagarakakshi: living in the ocean's whirlpool

Sagarambara: ocean-clad, earth

Sagarnemi: enriched by the ocean, earth

Sagari: of the ocean

Sahadevi: mighty goddess, protected by the goddesses

Sahajanya: produced together

Sahara: solace

Saheli: friend, attached with, small minaret

Sahimā: with snow

Sahitā: being near

Sahitrā: full of patience, enduring

Sahuri: full of heat, victorious, mighty, strong, earth

Saidā: fortunate

Sailukshā: goddess

Sairandhri: maid

Sajani: sweetheart, worthy companion

Sajeelā: decoration

Sakalasiddhi: possessing all perfection

Sakhi: generous, bountiful

Sakinā: peace of mind, tranquillity

Sākri: of Indra, wife of Indra

Sākshi: witness, with eyes

Sakuchanā: abashed

Salatā: soma juice-yielding plant

Sālikā: flute

Salochini: with beautiful eyes

Salomi: peace

Saloni: beautiful

Salwā: solace

Samā: of a peaceful nature, equanimity, similarity, a year

Samadu: daughter

Samajyā: fame, reputation

Samākhyā: fame, celebrity, name

Samālee: collection of flowers, noesgay

Samangini: complete in all parts

Samardhukā: prospering, succeeding, daughter

Samasti: reaching, attaining, totality, universe

Samatā: equality, fairness, benevolence, peaceful

Sambhuti: birth, origin, manifestation of night

Sambuddhi: perfect knowledge, perception

Samedi: moving one

Sameechi: praise, eulogy

Sameehā: desire, wish

Sameerā: entertaining companion

Samhitā: sacred book

Samishā: dart, javelin

Samiti: committee, herd, senate

Samati: harmony, agreeable, desire, wish, homage, knowledge, love, order, request

Sammā: sky

Sampad: perfection, attainment, accomplishment, blessing, fate, glory, success

Sampāngi: with a balanced body, a flower

Samyapradā: bestowing fortune

Sampatti: prosperity, accomplishment, being, concord, welfare

Sampreeti: complete satisfaction, joy, delight

Sampriyā: dear, beloved

Sampūjā: reverence, respect

Sampushṭi: perfect prosperity

Samrāj: ruling over all

Samrāṭ: universal queen

Samriddhi: prosperity, excellence, fortune, perfection, wealth

Samridhin: accomplished, perfect, blessed, happy, full of riches, Ganga

Samriti: meeting, coming together

Samudramahishi: chief wife of the ocean, Ganga

Samudranemi: surrounded by the ocean, earth

Samudrashree: beauty of the ocean, mermaid

Sāmudri: born of the ocean

Samyogitā: union with God

Sanah: radiant, resplendent, bright

Sānandā: full of pleasure, pleasant, joyful, Lakshmi

Sanātani: eternal, ancient, permanent, Durga, Lakshmi, Saraswati

Sanchārani: conveying, delivering a message, bringing near

Sandrā: defender of men

Sandhyā: twilight, meditation, union, holding together

Sāndhyakusumā: flower of the twilight, hibiscus

Sandhyārāga: colour of twilight, red colour of the evening sky

Sandhyāvali: period of twilight

Sangani: companion

Sangir: assent, promise

Sangeetā: music, symphony, chorus, concert

Sangeeti: concert, symphony

Sanheetā: collection of hymns

Sānikā: flute

Saniti: acquisition, procurement

Sanitrā: gift, offering

Sānjali: with hands, hollowed and joined in prayer

Sanjanā: one who joins, creator

Sanjiti: total victory

Sanjnā: well known, knowledge, perfect, agreement, clear understanding, consciousness, harmony, gesture, sign, token

Sanjogitā: attached, conjoined, related

Sankalpā: vow, with determination, resolution

Sankatā: remover of danger

Sankhyā: welfare, comfort, felicity, happiness, health

Sanmati: noble-minded

Sannam: farmer, kindness

Sannati: humility, bending down with humility

Sanojā: eternal

Sanoli: having self-penance, introspective

Sanraktā: red-coloured, beautiful, charming

Sanshati: doubting

Sansidhi: perfection, total accomplishement, success

Santani: continuing, making an uninterrupted line, harmony, music

Sāntanikā: stretching, cream, foam, cobweb, sword blade

Santāniki: made of kalpa tree flower

Santati: continuity, offspring, progeny, race

Santoshā: content, satisfied, pleased

Santoshi: contented, satisfied

Santushṭi: total satisfaction, contentment

Sānumati: mountain

Sanvitti: knowledge, harmony, intellect, understanding

Sanvritti: fulfilment, being, becoming, existing, happening

Sanjuktā: relating to, conjoined, united

Saparyā: worship, adoration, homage

Sapnā: dream

Saptajit: conquering the, elements earth, water, fire, air, ether, mind, ego

Sārā: solid, best, firm, excellent, hard, precious, valuable

Saraghā: having colour, passionate, impassioned, precious, valuable

Saraghā: beech tree

Saralā: straight, correct, honest, right, simple

Saramā: fleet-footed

Sārangā: lute, fiddle

Sārangi: spotted doe, a musical inistrument

Sarani: path, road

Saranyā: protector, shelter-provider, Durga

Saranyu: nimble, fleet-footed, quick

Sarasākshi: lotus-eyed

Saraswāni: sweet-voiced

Saraswati: area full of pools, full of essences, river goddess, goddess of learning and music

Saraigū: fast-moving, air, wind

Sargini: made of parts

Saridvarā: best of rivers, Ganga

Sārikā: mynah bird, confidante, Durga

Sarit: river, stream, Durga

Saritā: moving, river, stream

Sarojini: abounding in lotuses

Sarūpā: uniform, beautiful, handsome, embodied, similar

Sarvā: complete, perfect, whole

Sarvamangalā: universally, auspicious, Durga, Lakshmi

Sarvāni: omnipresent, perfect, Durga

Sarvapā: drinking everything

Sarvasahā: all-enduring, earth

Sarvasangā: going with all

Sarvāstrā: with all weapons

Sarvayashā: famous among all

Sarveshā: goddess of all

Sarveshi: desired by all

Sarvikā: universal, all, entire, whole

Sashrikā: having beauty, grace, fortune, lovely, splendid

Sashthi: praise, hymn, Durga

Sati: truthful, virtuous, faithful, Durga

Sāti: gift, offering, obtaining, gaining

Satpreetikā: beloved of truth

Sattvikā: of true essence, energetic, pure, spirited, true, vigorous, Durga

Satvanti: full of truth, faithful

Sātvati: pleasant, delighted

Satvati: truthful, faithful

Saumyā: moon-related, calm, pearl, gentle, Durga

Savitā: sun

Sāvitri: daughter of Daksha

Seema: border, limit

Selimā: peace

Semanti: white rose

85

Semantikā: white rose

Senjitā: vanquishing armies

Sevā: worship, devotion, homage, reverence

Sevati: white rose

Shabarā: spotted, variegated

Shabari: variegated

Shābhramati: full of water, cloudy

Shabnam: dew

Shacchandrikā: wonderful moonlight

Shachi: might, aid, farmer, grace, dexterity, kindness, skill

Shachikā: graceful, kind, skilled, dextrous

Shagufā: bud, blossom

Shakirā: grateful

Shailajā: daughter of the mountain, Parvati

Shailakanyā: daughter of the mountain, Parvati

Shailasa: dweller of mountains, Parvati

Shailendrajā: daughter of the mountains, Ganga

Shaili: carved in rock, custom, habit, style, visage

Shilyā: mountains

Shaivālini: river

Shaivi: prosperity, auspiciousness

Shākāmbari: herb-nourishing, Durga

Shākini: goddess of herbs, helpful, powerful, Parvati

Shakti: power, ability, energy, might, strength, Durga

Shaktimati: powerful

Shaktiyashas: with a lot of fame

Shakuni: auspicious object, lucky omen

Shakunikā: a bird

Shakuntikā: small bird

Shalabhā: grasshopper, locust

Shalada: procurer of spear

Shalākā: small stick, needle

Shalavati: owning a house, housewife, lady of the house

Shalina: courteous, fennel

Shalini: with a fixed abode, established, domestic, modest, shy, settled

Shalmalini: red silkcotton tree

Shama: calm, peaceful, tranquil, lamp

Shamani: tranquillity, peace

Shamani: calming one, night

Shambhari: blue-flowering sacred grass, Durga

Shambhu: helpful, kind, generous

Shambhupriya: dear to Shiva, Durga

Shammeha: peaceful

Shamilee: containing fire, garland

Shamira: chameli flower

Shampa: lightning

Shandili: collector

Shankara: causer of tranquillity

Shankari: wife of Shankar (Shiva)

Shankha: flute

Shankhadhaval: as white as a conchshell, jasmine

Shankhalika: flawless, as perfect as a conchshell

Shankhamukta: conchshell and pearl conjoined, mother of pearl

Shankarini: having branches, supreme among branches, best, excellent

Shankhyauthika: collection of conchshells, garland of jasmine

Shankini: mother of pearls

Shansha: praise, blessing, charm, invocation, wish, recitation

Shansita: desired, longed for, wished, celebrated

Shanta: calm, peaceful

Shanti: tranquillity, peace

Shantidevi: goddess of peace

Shantivā: bearer of peace, friendly, kind, beneficent

Shārada: lute bearer, veena bearer, Durga

Shāradamani: jewel among lutes, the best lute

Sharadashree: beauty of autumn

Sharadayāmini: night in autumn

Shāradi: autumn, day of full moon, modest, sky

Sharadi: as lovely as autumn

Shāradikā: autumnal

Shāradvati: with a lute, autumnal

Shārman: a fair share

Sharojyotsnā: autumnal moonshine

Sharani: protecting, defending, housing, earth

Sharāvati: full of reeds

Sharee: bird, arrow

Sharmi: industrious

Sharmilā: shy

Sharmishtha: most fortunate

Sharvā: Shiva's wife, Parvati

Sharvāni: night

Shashankvati: like the moon

Shashi: hare-marked, an apsara, moon

Shashibhās: moonbeam

Shashikalā: part of the moon, like the moon

Shashikāntā: beloved of the moon, while lotus

Shashilekhā: a part of the moon

Shashimukhi: moon-faced

Shashini: containing the moon, a part of the moon

Shashiprabhā: moonlight

Shashirashmi: moonlight

Shashthi: praise, hymn, Durga

Shāsti: praise, hymn

Shatadalā: with a 100 petals, white rose

Shatadruti: flowing in branches

Shatakārā: knower of 100 skills

Shatākshi: 100-eyed, night, Durga, dill

Shatapadmā: lotus with 100 petals, consisting of 100 lotuses, beautiful, loving, soft, tender

Shataparvā: with 100 parts

Shataprabhā: radiant, brilliant, lustrous

Shatapushkarā: consisting of 100 blue lotuses

Shatapushpā: consisting of 100 flowers, extremely beautiful, with a fragrant body

Shatarūpā: with a 100 forms

Shātodarā: slender-waisted

Shatrunjayā: conquering enemies

Shatvari: night

Shaylā: palace, fairy

Shāymā: sleeping goddess, Durga, Yamuna

Sheechi: flame, glow

Sheelā: calm, tranquil, good-natured

Sheelavati: virtuous, ethical

Sheephālikā: coral jasmine tree

Sheetalā: cold, cool, calm, gentle, passionate, moon

Sheetalatā: cooling power

Sheetamanjari: blossom of the cold, coral jasmine tree

Sheetashi: cold eater

Sheetikā: coldness

Sheetoshnā: cold and hot

Shelā: musical

Shemushi: intellect, wisdom, understanding

Shephāli: like drowsy bees, very fragrant, coral jasmine tree

Shephālikā: a fruit of mycanthes (coral tree)

Shevā: prosperity, happiness, homage

Shevalini: with a mass-like surface

Shibāni: Parvati

Shikhā: crest, flame, peak, pinnacle, ray of light, topknot

Shikhandi: crested, yellow, jasmine

Shikhandini: peahen

Shikharvasini: dwelling on a peak, Durga

Shikarini: eminent, excellent, Arabian jasmine

Shikra: skilful, able, artisitic, clever

Shila: rock

Shilavati: virtuous, moral

Shilpa: variegated

Shilpi: artisan

Shilpika: skilled in art

Shimida: giving work

Shinga: tinkle, jingle, tinkling of silver ornaments

Sinkhumar: porpoise

Shipha: whiplash, tuff of hair on crown of head

Shipra: cheeks, rose

Shirina: night

Shirley: country meadow

Shishugandha: with a youthful fragrance, double jasmine

Shiva: auspicious power, goddess of grace, final liberation, Parvati, Durga

Shivadevi: goddess of grace-prosperity-welfare

Shivaduti: Shiva's messenger, Durga

Shivadutika: Shiva's messenger

Shivakanta: beloved of Shiva, Durga

Shivakarini: doer of kind deeds, goddess of welfare, Durga

Shivakami: producer of prosperity

Shivali: beloved of Shiva, Parvati

Shivani: Parvati

Shivapriya: beloved of Shiva, Durga

Shivasundari: wife of Shiva, Parvati

Shivatmika: soul of Shiva, consisting of Shiva's essence

Shivika: palanquin

Shoba: pretty, lovely, beautiful

Shobanā: beautiful, turmeric

Shobhikā: brilliant, beautiful

Shobhini: graceful, wonderful

Shobhishtha: most beautiful, splendid

Shochayanti: inflaming

Shochi: flame

Shoki: night

Shonā: redness, fiery

Shornamani: red gem, ruby

Shonitā: red, saffron flower

Shraddhā: faith, loyalty, confidence, trust, reverence

Shravishthā: most famous

Shree: diffusing radiance, conjoining of beauty-grace-prosperity, grace, glory, light, majesty, power, splendour, Indian lotus

Shreyā: best, beautiful, excellent

Shrilātā: divine maiden

Shribhadrā: best among people

Shridā: given by Lakshmi, bestowing fortune

Shridevā: giver of fortune

Shridevi: goddess of prosperity, Lakshmi

Shriharā: excelling in all beauty

Shrihastini: in the hands of fortune, sunflower

Shrikā: born of Shree, prosperity, fortune, wealth, beauty

Shrikalā: a part of Lakshmi

Shrikāmyā: desirous of glory

Shrikanthikā: graceful-voiced

Shrilā: given by Lakshmi, beautiful, eminent, happy, prosperous

Shrilalitā: graceful, prosperous

Shrilatā: divine vine

Shrimangalā: goddess of prosperity

Shrimani: best among jewels, beautiful jewel

Shrimati: bearer of prosperity, beauty, divine, graceful, pleasant, royal, Spanish jasmine

Shrimukhi: with a radiant face

Shrina: night

Shrinandini: daughter of prosperity

Shrivani: divine speech

Shrividya: divine knowledge, Durga

Shriya: prosperity and happiness

Shringarika: love

Shringini: crested, cow, jasmine

Shrinjayi: giving victory

Shruta: famous, celebrated, glorious, heard, known

Shrutadevi: goddess of knowledge, Saraswati

Shrutakeerti: of well-known glory, famous

Shrutasoma: of the moon

Shrutashravas: listener of the scriptures

Shrutavati: favourably known

Shrutavinda: knower of the scriptures

Shruti: hearing, ear, knowledge of the *Vedas*

Shrutibuddhi: with knowledge of scriptures

Shubha: splendour, beauty, desire, decoration, light, lustre, ornament, assembly of gods

Shubhaga: going well, gracious, elegant

Shubhalochana: fair-eyed

Shubhamala: with a splendid garland

Shubhamayi: full of splendour, beautiful, splendid

Shubhananda: delighting in virtues

Shubhangi: with beautiful limbs

Shubhankari: doer of good deeds, virtuous, Parvati

Shubhasuchani: indicating good

Shaubhavaktra: of auspicious face

Shubhikā: garland of auspicious flowers

Shubhrā: radiant, Ganga

Shubhrāvati: fair-complexioned

Shubhrū: lovely browed woman

Shuchi: sacred, pure

Shuchimallikā: white vine, Arabian jasmine

Shuchimukhi: pure-face

Shuchintā: deep thought

Shuchismati: shining, radiant

Shuchismitā: with a pious smile

Shuddhā: clearness, purity, holiness, truth, Durga

Shukavāni: parrot-voiced

Shuki: parrot, bright, quick-witted, talkative

Shuklā: white, pure, bright, Saraswati

Shukti: beautiful verse, wise saying

Shuktimati: having oyster shells

Shūbadharā: bearing a spear, Shiva's wife, Durga

Shūladhāriṅi: holding a spear, Durga

Shūlini: armed with a spear, Durga

Shūraputrā: with a heroic son

Shveni: white

Shwetā: white

Shwetāmbarā: clad in white

Shweti: whiteness

Shwitrā: white

Shyāmā: dark, beautiful, blue, black

Shyamalā: dark, Durga

Shyeti: white

Shylāh: loyal to God, strong

Siddhalakshmi: perfect, fortune, Lakshmi

Siddhambā: blessed mother, Durga

Siddhānganā: an accomplished woman

Siddharthā: attainer of meaning, attainer of wealth

Siddhavati: achieving perfection

Siddhayogini: perfect yogini (fairy, magician)

Siddhi: accomplishment, acquisition of magical powers, fulfilment, luck, prosperity, success, Durga

Siddhidātri: bestower of perfection, Durga

Siddirūpini: goddess of achieving all

Siddhyāyikā: accomplisher, fulfiller, effector

Siham: arrows

Sila: ancient river

Simbala: a small pod, flower of Shalmali tree

Sindhu: ocean, sea, river

Sindhujā: ocean-born, Lakshmi

Sindhukanyā: daugher of the ocean, Lakshmi

Sidhumātri: mother of streams, Saraswati

Sinhamati: lion-hearted, courageous

Sinhi: lioness

Sinhikā: lioness

Sinhini: lioness

Sirinā: night

Sitā: white, sugar, moonlight, pretty woman

Sitārā: star

Sitasindhu: pure river, Ganga

Sitayāmini: moonlight

Smaradhwajā: bright moonlit night

Smaradūti: messenger of love

Smarani: act of remembering

Smerā: smiling, blossomed, apparent, evident, friendly

Smriti: remembrance, desire, code of laws, understanding, wish

Smritimālā: garland of memories

Snehā: affection, friendliness, love, tenderness

Snehal: full of affection

Snehalatā: vine of love

Snehamayi: loving

Snigdha: friendly, attached, agreeable, charming, glossy, intent, resplendent, shining, tender

Sohana: graceful, beautiful

Sohani: beautiful

Sohela: beautiful

Sohini: adorned, beautiful, splendid

Soma: soma plant, moonlike, beautiful

Somabha: like the moon

Somada: like a moon, bestower of tranquillity, producer of nectar

Somadevi: goddess of nectar

Somadhara: Milky Way, stream of soma

Somalata: creeper from which soma is extracted

Somali: beloved of the moon

Somashree: divine nectar

Somasuta: daughter of the moon

Somavati: containing soma

Sonila: moonlike, calm

Sona: gold

Sonakshi: golden-eyed, Parvati

Sonali: golden, Indian laburnum

Sonalika: golden

Soni: golden, beautiful

Sonia: Parvati

Sonika: with golden beauty

Sonya: wisdom

Sova: one's own

Spandana: heart-throb, pulsating beauty

Sparshanand: delighting the touch

Sragvini: wearing a wealth of flowers

Sravanti: flowing

Srikala: art of God

Srinjayi: giving victory

Sriti: path, road

Stava: praiser

Stāvarā: stable, steady, still, firm, constant, immovable

Sthira: strong-minded, earth

Streeratnā: jewel of a woman

Streetmā: complete woman

Stuti: praise, adulation, eulogy

Subakee: very strong, very powerful

Subāndhav: good friend

Subha: auspicious, glorious, splendid, Durga

Subhāgā: fortunate, rich

Subhāryā: prosperous lady, graceful lady

Subhāshani: soft-spoken

Subhashita: spoken well of

Subitā: comfort

Subudhi: of good intellect, clever, understanding, wise

Suchārā: very skilful, good performer

Suchara: with a beautiful gait

Suchhāyā: casting a beautiful shadow, beautiful, shining, brightly, splendid

Suchita: sacred, propitious

Suchitrā: well marked, having auspicious marks, distinguished, manifold, variegated

Sudāmā: generous

Sudāmini: as bright as lightning, wealthy, light

Sudanti: with good teeth

Sudarshanā: lovely in appearance, pleasing to eyes

Sudarshini: pretty, comely, lotus pond

Sudattā: well-given

Sudeshnā: born in a good place

Sudevi: real goddess

Sudhā: welfare, comfort, honey, ease, good drink, nectar, soma, water, lightning, Ganga

Sudānshuratna: jewel of the moon

Sudeshnā: King Virat's wife

96

Sudharmā: right path, follower of laws

Sudhi: intelligence, good sense

Sudheksha: beautiful, consecration, Lakshmi

Suditi: bright flame

Sudrishi: pretty, eye-pleasing, with beautiful eyes

Sugana: good attendant

Sugandha: fragrant, basil

Sugandhi: fragrant, blue lotus, small banana

Sugandhika: fragrant

Sugati: bliss, happiness, welfare

Sugātri: graceful, fair-limbed

Sugeshna: singing well

Sugreevi: with a beautiful neck

Suka: rejoicing

Suhāsini: smiling beautifully

Suhela: easily accessible

Suhita: beneficial, suitable

Sujasa: of good fame

Sujātā: well-born, noble, pretty

Sukala: good part, very skilled

Sukanthi: sweet-voiced

Sukanya: beautiful maiden

Sukeshi: with beautiful hair

Sukla: pleasure, comfort, ease, piety, virtue

Sukhada: giver of happiness, Ganga

Sukhavati: happy

Sukeerti: well praised, hymn of praise

Sukeshini: with beautiful hair

Sukhita: pleasure

Sukreeda: sporting

Sukrita: pious deed, doing good

Sukriti: auspiciousness, good conduct, kindness, virtue

Sukshi: beautiful verse, wise saying

Sukamari: very tender, very delicate, soft

Sukusumā: adorned with pretty flowers

Sulabhā: easily available, jasmine

Sulakshaṇā: with auspicious marks, fortunate, with good qualities

Sulakshmi: divine Lakshmi, divine wealth

Sulakshini: beautiful woman

Sulekhā: having auspicious line, fortunate

Sulochanā: with beautiful eyes

Sulochitā: very red

Sulomā: with beautiful hair

Sumadātmajā: daughter of passion

Sumadhyā: graceful woman, slender-waisted

Sumālini: well garlanded

Sumāllikā: geese, beautiful shuttle

Sumanā: beautiful, charming, lovely, wheat, Spanish jasmine

Sumangatā: auspicious

Sumangali: auspicious, Parvati

Sumantikā: Indian white rose

Sumati: good mind, devotion, generosity, kindness

Sumārali: garland of flowers

Sumāyā: with excellent plans

Sumehrā: beautiful face

Sumirā: much remembered, overtly praised

Sumitā: with a balanced form, with a beautiful body, well measured

Sumitrā: nice friend, having many friends

Sumnāvari: bringing joy

Sumonā: quiet, calm

Sumrini: rosary

Sumukhi: bright faced, learned, lovely, pleasing

Sumuṇḍika: with a good head, sensible

Sunakshatra: born under an auspicious constellation

Sunami: well-named

Sunanda: pleasing, delighting, Parvati

Sunandi: pleasing, delighting

Sunaya: very first, well conducted

Sunayana: with beautiful eyes

Sundaravati: having beauty

Sundari: beautiful

Suneeta: of blue colour, very dark

Suneelima: bright blue, dark

Suneeti: good conduct, wisdom, discretion

Sunehri: golden

Suniksha: one with beautiful ornaments

Sunita: well conducted, civil, polite, well behaved

Sunitha: moral, righteous, virtuous, well disposed

Sunvita: joy, exultation, gladness, kindness

Suparna: with beautiful leaves, Parvati

Suphulla: with beautiful blossoms

Suprabha: very bright, beautiful, splendid

Suprabhat: illuminated by dawn, morning prayer

Supraja: with many children

Suprasada: auspicious, gracious, propitious

Suprateekini: with beautiful form

Supratishtha: well established, consecration, famous, glorious, installation

Suprayoga: well managed, well practised, dextrous

Suprema: very loving

Supriti: great joy, great delight

Supriya: very dear, lovely

Supunya: bearer of good deeds, of great religious merit

Supushpa: with beautiful flowers

Surā: wine, spirituous liquor

Surabhi: sweet-smelling, agreeable, beautiful, beloved, charming, famous, pleasing, wise, shining, virtuous, basil, jasmine, earth

Surabhū: born of the gods

Surādevi: goddess of wine

Surajā: born of the gods

Surajani: beautiful night

Surakāmini: desired by the gods

Suralā: bringer of gods, Ganga

Suranyā: very beautiful

Suranā: gay, joyous, making a pleasing sound

Surananda: joy of the gods

Surāngana: celestial woman

Surapriyā: dear to the gods

Surasā: of good essence, elegant, lovely, sweet, well flavoured, basil, Durga

Surastri: celestial woman

Surasū: mother of gods

Surasundari: celestial beauty, Durga

Surathā: with a good chariot

Suratnā: possessing rich jewels

Suravāhini: river of the gods, Ganga

Suravalli: vine of the gods, basil

Suravāni: earth

Suravarā: best among the gods

Suravilāsini: heavenly mymph, apsara

Surbalā: female deity

Sureeli: in time

Sureetā: melodious

Surejyā: worshipped by the gods, sacred basil

Surekhā: having beautiful lines, auspicious, fortunate

Surenū: very small, dust particle, an atom

Sureshi: supreme goddess, Durga

Sūri: wife of the sun

Suri: goddess

Surmyā: good-looking

Surochanā: much liked, beautiful, enlightening

Surohi ni: beautifully red

Surtā: divine truth

Suruchā: bright light, with fine tastes

Suruchi: taking pleasure in

Surukhi: with a pretty face

Surūpā: well formed, beautiful, lovely, Spanish jasmine

Surūpikā: well formed, beautiful

Sūryā: wife of Sun god

Suryabhā: as bright as the sun

Sūryajā: born of the sun

Sūryakalā: a part of the sun

Sūryakānti: sunshine, sunlight

Sūryalochanā: eye of the sun, with bright eyes

Sūryamukhi: sun-faced, bright face, sunflower

Sūryāni: wife of the sun

Sūryaprabhā: as bright as the sun

Sūryashobhā: sunshine, as beautiful as the sun

Suryashree: divine sun

Sushmā: exquisite beauty, splendour

Susangatā: good companion, easily attainable

Sunshāntā: perfectly calm

Susatyā: always truthful

Sushilā: well disposed, good tempered

Sushilikā: of good character, a bird

Sushobhana: very charming, very graceful

Sushravā: very famous, well known

Sushree: very rich, extremely splendid

Sushubhā: very auspicious, very beautiful

Sushyāmā: very beautiful, very dark

Susimā: with the hair well parted

Susmitā: with a pleasant smile

Suswarā: sweet-voiced

Sutā: begotten, daughter

Sutanu: slender, delicate

Sutārā: very bright, twinkling star, cat's eye

Sutārakā: with beautiful water, sparking water

Sutrāmā: protecting well, earth

Surachā: speaking well

Surachani: always speaking well, lute

Suvali: graceful

Suvāmā: beautiful woman

Surachalā: abode of a glorious life

Suvarchas: full of life, very glorious

Suvarṇā: golden-linked, gold, turmeric

Suvarṇarekhā: golden line

Suvārtā: good news, bringer of good tidings

Suvāsini: fragrance

Suvāsu: fragrant

Suvedā: very intelligent, very knowledgeable, know of scriptures

Suveṇā: with beautifully plaited hair

Suvithi: good knowledge, divine being

Suvratā: very religious, virtuous wife

Suvitā: well behaved, good, virtuous

Suvyūhā: halo

Suyashā: very famous

Suyashas: very famous

Swadhā: self-power

Swadhi: well minded, thoughtful

Swakriti: good looking

Swamini: lady of the house

Swapnā: dream

Swapnasundari: dreamgirl

Swarā: goddess of music, goddess of musical notes

Swaradevi: knower of music, goddess of music

Swarbhānavi: daughter of the divine, daughter of the sun

Swareñu: beautiful note

Swargangā: Milky Way, celestial Ganga

Swarña: golden

Swarnalatā: golden wine

Swarnamālā: golden necklace

Swarñāmbhā: white light, golden light

Swarñapadmā: having golden lotuses, celestial Ganga

Swarnapushpikā: golden flower, jasmine

Swarnarekhā: golden streak

Swārshā: celestial, bestowing light

Swarūpā: beautiful

Swarneethi: heavenly path, abode of music

Swaryoshit: celestial woman

Swasti: well being, success, fortune

Swasū: self-created, earth

Swāti: one of the seven constellations, the star Arcturus

Swayamprabhā: self-shining

Swikriti: acceptance

T

Tabita: gazelle

Tadiprabha: flash of lightning

Tahirah: chaste, pure

Talakakshi: with green eyes

Talakhya: perfume

Talika: palm of the hand, nightingale

Talli: young, boat, youthful

Talsim: miracle, wonder, enchantment

Taluni: maiden

Tama: night

Tamaharini: dispeller of darkness

Tamasa: dark-coloured

Tamasi: night, sleep, Durga

Tamasvini: night

Tami: night

Tamra: copper-crested

Tamrajakshi: copper-eyed

Tamrakarni: ears of copper hue

Tamrapaksha: copper-hued

Tamrapami: with red leaves

Tamrarasa: of red juice

Tamravati: coppery

Tamrika: coppery

Tanu: beautiful, excellent

Tanubhava: daughter

Tanuja: born of the body, daughter

Tanulata: with a vine-like body, supple, slender

Tanushree: with a divine body

Tanveer: delicate woman

Tanuvi: slender woman

Tanvangi: slender-limbed

Tanvi: slender, delicate, beautiful, fine

Tanya: daughter

Tapanasuta: daugher of the sun, Yamuna

Tapanatanya: daughter of the sun

Tapanātmajā: daughter of the sun, Yamuna

Tāpani: heat

Tapanti: warming

Tapaswini: ascetic

Tapati: warming

Tāpi: heat, glow

Tārā: star, pupil of the eye, perfume, meteor, rocky

Tārābhūshā: adorned with stars, night

Tārādattā: given by the stars

Tāraka: falling star, meteor, star, eye

Tārakini: starry night

Taralā: spirituous liquor, bee

Tārāmati: with a glorious mind

Tārāmbā: mother star

Tārānā: song

Tarangini: full of waves, moving, restless

Tarani: boat, raft

Tārāpushpa: star blossom, jasmine

Tārāvali: multitude of stars

Tārāvati: surrounded by stars, Durga

Tārikā: belonging to the stars

Tāriṅi: enabling to cross over, saving, Durga

Tārinnerā: crossing over the water, possessing liberating quality

Taritā: forefinger, leader, Durga

Tarnijā: Yamuna

Tarpiṅi: satisfying, hibiscus, offering oblations

Tarulatā: vine

Taruni: young girl

Tarushi: victory

Tasli: comfort, peace

Tatikshā: endurance, patience

Tātripi: intensely satisfiying

Tātum: cheerful, joy-bringer

Tavishi: power, courage, heavenly virgin, strength, river, earth

Ṭawnie: little one, yellowish-brown

Teerthā: passage, ford, place of pilgrimage, way, sacred object, water

Teerthamayi: having pilgrimage centres

Teerthanemi: circumbulating carrying sacred objects the sacred place,

Teerthavali: pious, holy, flowing through a sacred place

Tejashree: with divine power, divine grace

Tejasvati: energetic, bright, glorious, splendid

Tejasvitā: nobility, radiance

Tejini: sharp, energetic, bright, whetstone, touchstone

Tejomayi: consisting of light, full of splendour

Tejovati: bright, sharp, splendid

Tejwanti: radiant

Thākuri: deity

Thanā: gratitude

Tharā: wealth

Thistle: plant with thorns

Tilabhavāni: beautiful dot, jasmine

Tilakā: type of necklace

Tilakalatā: ornamental vine

Tilakāvati: decorated

Tilikā: marked with sandalpaste

Tilla: preceder

Tilotamā: damsel of great beauty

Timi: fish

Timilā: a musical instrument

Tinā: illustrious, a river

Tintishā: a tree

Tipti: daughter of Sun god

Tishyarakshitā: protected by luck

Titikshā: endurance, patience

Titli: butterfly

Toshani: pleasing, satisfying, appeasing, gratifying, Durga

Tatalā: repetitive, Durga

Toyā: water

Toyaneevi: girdled by ocean, earth

Trayee: intellect, understanding

Treyā: treading the three paths

Triambikā: wife of three-eyed Shiva, Parvati

Tridhārā: stream with three tributaries, Ganga

Tridivā: heaven, cardamom

Trigartā: woman, pearl

Trihayani: returning in three years

Trijagati: mother of the three worlds, Parvati

Trijamā: night

Trijaṭā: with three locks of hair

Trikalā: of three pieces

Trilochanā: wife of the three-eyed Shiva, Parvati

Trinainā: Durga

Tripti: satisfaction

Tripurā: triply fortified, Durga

Triputā: threefold, Arabian jasmine, Durga

Trishalā: three-pointed

Trishnā: desire

Trishulini: wife of the trishul bearer, Durga

Triveni: triple-braided

Triyā: young woman

Triptā: contentment, satisfaction, Ganga

Tripti: contentment, satisfaction, water

Trishā: thirst

Trishlā: thirsting, deserving

Trishnā: thirst, desire

Trivali: blue lotus

Trudy: beloved

Truti: atom, a small part of time

Tudi: satisfying

Tuhi: cuckoo's cry

Tulasārini: quiver

Tulasi: matchless, sacred basil

Tūlini: cotton tree

Ṭully: peaceful

Tungā: strong, high, elevated

Tungabhadrā: very noble, sacred

Tungavenā: loving heights

Tungi: night, turmeric

Turavati: wind

Turi: painter's brush

Turuyā: superior powers

Tushā: longing, desire

Tushitā: pleased, satisfied

Tushti: satisfaction, contentment

Tuvikshtara: ruling strongly

Twaritā: swift, quick, expenditious, Durga

Tweshā: brilliant, glittering, vehement, impetuous

Twishā: light, splendour

Twishi: vehemence, brilliance, energy, light, splendour, impetuosity

U

Ucchadevatā: superior god, time personified

Ucchatā: superiority, height

Undadhisutā: daugher of the ocean, Lakshmi

Udalākāshyap : watering the earth, goddess of agriculture

Udankanyā: daugher of the ocean, Lakshmi

Udantikā: satisfaction, contentment

Udāramati: noble-minded

Udayanti: risen, excellent, virtuous

Udayati: daughter of the mountain

Udbhūti: emerging, appearance, existing, fortune-giver

Uddeepti: excited, inflamed

Udgeetā: sung, celebrated, extolled, hymn of the glory, ultimate song

Udgeeti: singing

Uditi: rising of the sun

Udu: water, star

Udvahā: carrying on, continuing, daughter

Udvahni: sparkling, gleaming

Udyati: raised, elevated

Ugrachārini: moving impetuously, Durga

Ugraduhitri: daughter of a powerful man

Ugrajit: victor of passion

Ujālā: shining, radiant, luminous

Ujāli: night

Ujjayati: winner, conqueror, victory

Ujjeshā: victorious

Ujjiti: victory

Ujjivati: brought to life, full of life, jubilant, optimist

Ujjeevayati: animated

Ujjwalā: splendour, clearness, brightness

Ujjwalitā: shining, lighted, flaming

Utharkā: praise of the sun, hymn of the sun

Uktasampadā: wealth of hymns

Ukthin: uttering verses, praising

Ukti: proclamation, idiom, expression, word, sentence, speech

Ulā: seaweed

Ulfāh: friendship, harmony, love

Ulimā: astute, wise

Ulkā: meteor, fire, torch, firebrand, falling from heaven

Ulkushi: meteor, firebrand

Ulūki: female owl

Ulūpi: with a charming face

Utūki: female falcon

Umā: splendour, fame, light, night, quiet, reputation, tranquillity, Parvati, Durga

Umaymā: young mother

Umlochā: with questioning eyes

Unā: one

Unaysā: friendly, affable

Uneṭṭe: crowned lamb

Unice: victory

Unnā: woman

Unmadā: with intoxicating beauty, passionate

Unmādini: bewitching, intoxicating

Unmukti: deliverance

Unnati: dignity, prosperity, progress, rising

Upabhuti: enjoyment

Upaḍā: gift, offering, benevolent

Upadhriti: ray of light

Upakārikā: protector

Upakoshā: like a treasure

Upamā: resemblance, equality, similarity

Upanayikā: fit for an offering

Upaneeti: initiation

Upāsanā: devotion, homage, worship

Upashamtā: tranquillity, patience

Upashruti: listening attentively

Upāsti: worship, adoration

Upavenā: with small tributaries

Uraniā: heavenly

Uranitā: precious metal

Uriānā: gracious light

Urilyn: beautiful light

Urishṭa: tree

Urity: purity

Ūrjā: energy, vigour, strength, breath, food, heartborn, power, water

Ūrjani: belonging to energy

Urjaswati: vigorous, powerful, juicy

Urjjasvati: full of energy, strong

Ūrmi: ripple, wave, light

Ūrmikā: wave, hum of bees, finger ring

Ūrmilā: of the waves of passion, beautiful, enchanting

Ūrmyā: wavy, night

Ūrnā: woollen, warm, ever excited

Urooj: height, exaltation

Ursullā: female bear

Urukeerti: of far-reaching fame

Urunjirā: pleaser of heart, hear-winning

Urushā: granting much, producing plentiful

Urutā: greatness, vastness

Uruvi: great, broad, excellent, large, spacious, earth

Urvanā: fairy

Uravarā: fertile soil, earth

Urvashi: widely, extending, Ganga

Urvi: wide one, earth

Urvijā: Sita

Ushā: daybreak, dawn, morning light

Ushamā: summer

Ushas: dawn, morning light

Ushalākshi: dawn-eyed, large-eyed, with piercing, eyes

Ushi: wish

Ushira: fragrant root of a sacred plant

Ushnā: with desire

Ushānā: desire, wish, plant of some juice

Ushasi: twilight

Ushijā: desire-born, available, charming, deserving, desirable, wishing, zealous

Ushikā: worshipper of dawn

Usrā: morning light, brightness, earth

Usri: dawn, morning light, daybreak

Utala: agile, quick

Ūti: help, enjoyment, kindness, protection

Utinā: anointed

Uthalikā: yearning for glory, bud, wave

Uthalitā: unbounded, blossoming, brilliant, opened, loosened

Utkanikā: desire, yearning

Utkānti: excessive, splendour

Utkarikā: of precious material

Utkarshini: attributes

Utkārthini: fulfilling one's ambitions

Utkāshanā: giving orders, commanding

Utkhalā: perfume

Utkrashitā: excellence, superiority

Utshiptikā: lifted, crescent-shaped earring for upper ear

Utkūjā: cooing note of bird

Utpalā: filled the lotuses

Utpalākshi: lotus-eyed, Lakshmi

Utpalamālā: garland of lotus flowers

Utpalāvati: made of lotuses

Utpalini: collection of lotuses

Uttamā: best, affectionate, excellent

Uttamikā: best worker

Uttarā: higher, upper, northern, future, result

Uttarikā: crossing over, emerging, conveying, delivering, boat

Uttejini: exciting, animating

Uvā: breath of life

Uzimā: great

Uzmā: the greatest

Uzuri: beauty

V

Vāchā: speech, oath, voice, word, sacred text

Vāchaknavi: with the power of speech, speaker, orator, eloquent

Vadhusarā: mobile woman

Vāgdevi: goddess of speech, Saraswati

Vageeshwari: goddess of speech, Saraswati

Vāhini: body of force, army

Vahnijāyā: conqueror of fire

Vahnikanyā: daughter of fire, air, wind

Vahnipriyā: beloved of fire

Vahnishwari: goddess of fire, Lakshmi

Vahyakā: chariot

Vaidagdhi: grace, beauty

Vaidehi: princess of the Videhas, Sita

Vaidhriti: with a similar disposition, properly adjusted

Vaijayanti: gift of victory, flag, garland of victory, banner

Vaijayantikā: bestowing victory, banner, flag, pearl necklace

Vaijayantimālā: garland of victory

Vaikunthā: without hindrance, abode of the absolute

Vaimitrā: friend of the universe

Vairāgi: free from passions

Vaishāli: the great

Vaishālini: daughter of the great

Vaishnavi: worshipper of Vishnu

Vaitarani: helper in crossing over to the other world

Vaivasvati: belonging to the sun, Yamuna

Vajrā: mighty, strong, hard, Durga

Vajradehi: diamond-bodied

Vajrajivālā: shining like lightning

114

Vajramālā: with a diamond necklace

Vajrashree: divine diamond

Vajravalli: useful vine, sunflower

Vāka: word, speech, recitation, text

Vākapradā: giver of speech, Saraswati

Vākini: reciter

Vakshanā: nourisher, bed of a river, refreshing

Vakshani: strengthening

Vakshi: strength, nourishment, flame

Vakti: speech

Vala: chosen

Valashiphā: curled hair

Valyā: coiled, armlet, bracelet, ring

Vālguki: very beautiful

Vālini: with a tail, constellation Ashwini

Vallabhā: beloved

Vallaki: lute

Vallari: cluster of blossoms, creeper, Sita

Vallarika: vine

Vallāri: vine

Valhi: creeper, vine, lightning, earth

Vallika: covered with vines, covered with greenery

Vāma: beautiful, Durga, Lakshmi, Saraswati

Vāmākshi: fair-eyed

Vāmālochanā: four-eyed

Vāmini: bringing wealth, short

Vāmanikā: small

Vāmika: situated on the left side

Vanachandrika: moon rays, of the forest, jasmine

Vanajā: forest-born, water-born, sylvan, blue lotus

Vanajākshi: blue lotus-eyed

Vanajāyatā: resembling a lotus

Vanajyotsni: light of the jungle, jasmine

Vanalatā: creeper of the forest, vine

115

Vanalika: of the forest, sunflower

Vanamāla: garland of the forest, garland of flower, flower braid

Vanamālika: garland of the forest, garland of wild flowers

Vanamāleeshā: desired by the forest gardener

Vanamalli: wild, jasmine

Vanamallika: jasmine

Vanāmbikā: mother of the forest

Vanapushpā: flower of the forest, wild flower

Vanarashmi: light of the forest, ray of light

Vanasorojini: lotus of the forest, wild cotton plant, collection of wild lotuses

Vanashobhanā: water, beautifying, lotus

Vanathi: of the forest

Vānchā: desire, wish

Vandanā: adoration, praise, worship, prayer

Vandanikā: praised, honoured

Vanditā: praised, worshipped

Vandyā: praiseworthy, adorable

Vāni: desire, wish

Vānichi: speech

Vānimayi: goddess of speech, Saraswati

Vānini: soft-voiced, intriguing woman

Vānishree: divine speech, Saraswati

Vanitā: desired, wished for, loved, woman

Vanjulā: a cow full of milk

Vankshu: arm

Vanmayi: goddess of speech, Saraswati

Vansā: goddess

Vanshā: offspring, daughter, lineage, bamboo

Vanshadhārā: carrying on the race

Vanshalakshmi: family fortune

Vanshi: flute, pipe, artery

Vanshikā: flute

Vanu: eager, zealous, friend

Vānyā: sylvan

Vaprā: garden bed

Vapu: body

Vapushā: embodied, beauty, very beautiful, handsome, nature

Vapushi: embodied, wonderfully beautiful

Vapushmati: having a form, beautiful

Vapushṭamā: best among the embodied, wonderfully beautiful

Varā: boon, benefit, blessing, choice, gift, reward, Parvati

Varadā: giver of boons, girl, maiden

Varajākshi: with lotus eyes

Varālikā: goddess of power, Durga

Varaṇā: encompassing, surrounding, enclosing, rampant

Varānanā: with a beautiful face

Varanāri: best woman

Vārānāshi: granting boons

Vāranganā: beautiful

Vārāngi: with a beautiful body

Varāngi: with a graceful form, turmeric

Varapakshīnā: well feathered

Varapradā: granting wishes

Vararohā: elegant, fine, handsome, fine rider

Varastree: noble woman

Varasyā: desire, request, wish

Varavamini: with a beautiful complexion, Durga, Lakshmi, Saraswati

Vāree: rich in presents, goddess of speech, water, Saraswati

Varee: stream, river

Varenyā: desirable, Shiva's wife, saffron

Vargā: belonging to a set or group

Varijakshā: lotus-eyed

117

Varishā: monsoon

Varivasyā: devotion, honour, obedience, service

Varjā: water-born, lotus

Varnapushpi: coloured flower, amaranth lily

Varnikā: of fine colour, fine gold, purity of gold

Varoyashit: beautiful woman

Varshā: rain, monsoon

Vārshikā: belonging to the monsoon, yearly, jasmine

Vārtā: news, tidings, intelligence

Varunā: goddess of water

Varunāni: water-born, Lakshmi

Vāruṇi: of water, resembling water, wine, liquor

Varūthini: multitude, army, troop

Varūtri: protector

Vanyā: treasure, wealth, chosen, valuable

Vashā: obedient, willing

Vāsanā: knowledge from past experience, desire, fancy, imagination, inclination, motion

Vasantajā: born in spring, jasmine

Vasantakusum: spring flower

Vasantalatā: vine of spring

Vasantalekhā: spring-written, spring-born

Vasantasenā: with spring as army commander, as charming as spring

Vasantashree: beauty of spring

Vāsanti: of the spring season, light yellow, saffron

Vasantikā: goddess of spring

Vasāti: dawn

Vasavadattā: enticing, fragrance-born, given by Indra

Vāsavi: daughter of the all-pervading

Vasāvi: treasury

Vashitā: bewitching

Vasita: woman

Vasordhārā: stream of wealth, celestial Ganga

Vastri: shining, illumining

Vastu: dawn, morning

Vasu: light, radiance

Vasudā: granting wealth, earth

Vasudāmā: controlling the divine beings

Vasudattā: given by the gods

Vasudevā: goddess of wealth

Vasudhā: producing wealth, earth, Lakshmi

Vasudharā: bearing wealth

Vasudhārini: bearer of treasures, earth

Vasudhiti: having wealth

Vasulakshmi: divine goddess of wealth

Vasumati: having treasure, earth

Vasundhara: abode of weath, containing wealth

Vasundharesha: wife of the lord of the earth

Vasundhareyi: daughter of the earth, Sita

Vasuprabhā: divine light

Vāsurā: valuable, night, earth, woman

Vasushree: divine grace

Vasvi: divine night

Vasvoksārā: essence of divine waters

Vātansā: garland, ring, crest

Yātarūpā: with the form of wind, subtle, transparent

Vātikā: Ved Vyas's wife

Vatshā: child-loving, affectionate, devoted, loving

Vatsamitrā: friend of children, friend of calves

Vatū: speaker of truth

Vayā: branch, twig, child, power, strength, vigour

Vayodhā: invigorating, strengthening, refreshing

Vayuṅā: moving, alive, active, mark, aim, goals, wisdom, knowledge

Vayuvega: swift as the wind

Vedā: well-known, famous, meritorious, pious

Vedabhā: obtained from knowledge

Vedajanani: mother of the Vedas, Gayatri mantra

Vedamātri: mother of the Vedas, Saraswati, Gayatri

Vedana: knowledge, perception, pain, discomfort

Vedāsini: carrying wealth

Vedashree: beauty of Vedas

Vedashruti: heard about in the Vedas, famous in Vedas

Vedavati: knower of the Vedas

Vedeshvā: born of the sacred texts

Vedhasyā: worship, piety

Vedi: knowledge, altar, science

Vedikā: making known, seal ring, restoring to consciousness

Vedini: knowing, feeling, announcing

Vedyā: knowledge

Veeksha: knowledge, intelligence

Veena: lightning, lute

Veendu: dot, point, intelligence, wisdom

Veerā: brave, excellent, heroic, powerful, strong, wise

Veerabāla: brave maiden

Veerāni: brave woman

Veerendri: goddess of the brave

Veerikā: possessed with bravery

Veerini: of whom the brave are born, mother of some

Veerudhā: sprouting, formed, grown

Veeryā: vigour, energy, strength

Veeryavati: powerful

Veeti: enjoyment, fire, light, lustre

Vega: falling star

Vegavahini: flowing fast

Vegavati: rapid

Vemā: goddess

Veṇikā: constantly flowing

Verity: truth

Vibhāsanā: glitter, shine

Vidipitā: lighted

Vidhuvati: beautiful woman

Vidnā: fate, destiny

Vidyā: spiritual knowledge, learning

Vidyādevi: goddess of learning

Vidyādhari: learning knowledge

Vidyāgauri: goddess of knowledge

Vidyāvadhū: presiding goddess over learning

Vidyāvati: learned

Vidyotā: consisting of lightning, glittering, shining

Vidyudvalli: flash of lightning

Vidyudvarṇā: lightning coloured

Vidyudyotā: with the brightness of learning

Vidyulatā: creeper of lightning

Vidyullekhā: streak of lightning

Vidyutā: lightning, dawn, flashing thunderbolt

Vidyutparṇā: having lightning as wings

Vidyutprabhā: flashing like lightning

Vihā: heaven

Vikasatikā: gentle laughter, smiling

Vijarā: ever young

Vijayā: victorious, triumphant, Durga

Vijayshantikā: finally victorious

Vijayshree: glory of victory

Vijayvati: victorious

Vijiti: victory, triumph

Vijittāri: vanquisher

Vikachashree: with radiant beauty

Vikāshini: shining, radiant, illuminant

Vikhyāti: fame, celebrity

Vikrānti: all-pervading, heroism, might, prowess, strength

Vikunthā: inward glance, penetration, mental concentration

Vilāsmayi: playful, graceful, charming

Vilāsanti: flashing, glittering, shining

Vilāsini: radiant, charming, lively, playful, shining, Lakshmi

Vilochanā: beautiful eyes

Vilohitā: deep red

Vimala: flawless, stainless, clear, pure, sacred, spotless, bright

Vimalamati: pure in heart

Vimi: goddess

Vimochani: freedom, emancipation, liberation

Vinamratā: gentleness, modesty, politeness

Vinata: humble, a bower

Vinati: prayer, humility, entreaty, modesty

Vinay: politeness

Vināyvati: polite, modest, gentle

Vineeti: modesty, good conduct, training

Vindā: auspicious time

Vindu: water drop

Vinodini: humorous, witty

Vinodita: amused, delighted, diverted

Vipā: speech

Vipanchi: remover of troubles

Vipāshā: unbound, chainless

Vipodhā: inspiring

Vipachitti: sagacious

Vipsa: repetition, succession

Vipula: great, abundant, large, earth

Vipulekshanā: large-eyed

Virajā: clean, dust-free, pure

Virajini: brilliant, splendid, queen

Virendri: goddess of the brave

Virochanā: shining upon, illuminating

Virūpā: manifold, variegated, altered

Vishālā: large, extensive, spacious, wide

Vishalākshi: large-eye, Durga

Vishalyā: relieved from pain

Vishirā: with no prominent veins

Vishnu: omnipresent

Vishnumati: with omnipresent intelligence

Vishnumāyā: illusion of Vishnu, Durga

Vishnupriyā: beloved of Vishnu, wax flower, Lakshmi

Vishobhaginā: prosperous, Saraswati

Vishokā: exempted from grief

Vishruti: fame, celebrity

Vishtāreni: large, might, extensive, expansive, spreading

Vishuddhi: purity, sacredness, virtue, perfect knowledge, holiness

Vishwā: earth

Vishwadhāriṅi: abode of the universe, all-maintaining, earth

Vishwadhenā: cow of the universe, all-feeding, earth

Vishwagandhā: fragrance of the universe, fragrance, all-pervading, earth

Vishwamalā: enchanting the universe, all-delighting, all-consuming

Vishwambhari: feeding the universe, all-bearing, earth

Vishwamukhi: of the universe

Vishwapāvani: pious in the universe, sacred basil

Vishwapūjitā: worshipped by all, sacred basil

Vishwaruchi: illuminator of the universe, all-glittering

Vishwarūpā: with the form of the universe, multi-coloured, many-coloured

Vishwarūpikā: with the form of the universe

Vishwarūpiṇi: with the form of the universe, creator of universe

Vishwasahā: all-enduring

Vishwavati: possessing the universe, universal, Ganga

Vishweshā: lady of the universe, desired by all

Vitanā: extension, abundance, heap, oblation, performance, plenty

Vitolā: very calm

Vittadā: giver of wealth

Vitti: acquisition, gain, finding

Vivandishā: wish to worship

Vivasvati: shining forth, diffusing light

Vivian: full of life

Vivianne: gracious, vibrant

Viviette: vibrant, full of life

Vivitsā: desire for knowledge

Vivyan: vibrant, full of life

Viyadgangā: celestial ganga, galaxy

Voletā: veiled one

Vonessā: butterfly

Vreni: verity, truth

Vrichayā: searching

Vriddhā: great, eldest, experienced, large, learned, wise

Vriddhakanyā: daughter of preceptor

Vrindā: swarm, flock, cluster of flowers, all, many, choruses of singers, heap, sacred basil

Vrishakā: cow

Vrittamallikā: encircling creeper, jasmine

Vritti: existence, being, moral conduct, state

Vūrnā: chosen, selected

Vyāpti: accomplishement, attainment, omnipresence

Viyashṭi: attainment, individuality, singleness, success

Vumā: mother

124

Vyatibha: shining forth

Vyeni: variously hued, dawn

Vyomaganga: celestial Ganga

Vyomini: celestial

Vyushti: first gleam of dawn, beauty, felicity, grace, fruit, reward, prosperity

Waheedā: exquisite, beautiful

Waiyā: beautiful pearl

Wamikā: a goddess

Wanā: turtle dove

Wendy: fair

Widjan: ecstacy

Wynne: light-complexioned

Yādavi: woman of the Yadava tribe, Durga

Yadunandini: daughter of the Yadus

Yadvā: perception, intelligence, mind

Yagaseni: daughter of fire

Yahvā: heaven and earth, flowing water

Yahvat: everflowing waters

Yajā: worshipper, sacrificer

Yajnikā: offering to God

Yakshāngi: alive, speedy

Yakshi: female protector of forests, quick, speedy, supernatural being

Yakshini: another name for Yakshi

Yamakālindi: blossoming

Yamalā: twin

Yamamā: a valley

Yamee: elder twin sister, pair, couple, brace

Yāmee: motion, progress, path, road, carriage, course

Yāminā: right and proper

Yāmini: consisting of watches, night

Yāmyā: night

Yashasvati: famous, illustrious

Yashasvini: beautiful, famous, illustrious, splendid

Yashodā: conferring fame, Durga

Yashodevi: goddess of fame and beauty

Yashodhā: conferring splendour and fame

Yashodharā: maintaining fame and glory

Yasholekhā: narrative of glorious deeds

Yashomati: having fame

Yashovati: possessing fame and glory

Yashṭikā: string of pearls

Yāsmin: fasmine

Yati: restraint, control, guidance

Yātudhāni: magician, conjurer

Yeḍḍā: singing

Yogā: total, meditation, conjunction

Yogadeepikā: light of meditation

Yogamāyā: magical power of abstract meditation, Durga

Yoganidrā: meditation sleep

Yogaratnā: magical jewel

Yogasiddhā: yoga-perfected

Yogatārā: chief star of a constellation

Yogavati: joined, united, versed in yoga

Yogeshwari: adept in yoga, Durga

Yogin: meditator, ascetic, devotee

Yogini: with magical power, fairy, sorceress

Yogitā: enchanted, bewitched, wild

Yoninā: little dove

Yori: reliable

Yoshā: young woman, maiden

Yoshanā: girl, young woman

Yoshi: blessed

Yoshidratnā: jewel among women

Yoshino: respectful, good

Yoshitā: woman, wife

Young: eternal wealth

Yovelā: rejoicing

Yubhikā: numerous

Yue: moon

Yugal: pair

Yugandharā: bearing an era, earth

Yuliānā: downy-haired

Yuliyā: downy-haired

Yulisā: truth, noble

Yuki: blessed, snow

Yuko: gracious child

Yumnā: good fortune, successful

Yumi: beautiful

Yun: cloud

Yusrā: prosperous

Yūthikā: multitude, white jasmine

Yuvateeshṭa: yellow jasmine

Yuvikā: jasmine

Yveṭte: yew tree

Yvonniṭā: yew tree, gracious

Zāfeerā: firm

Zāfinā: victorious

Zafirā: successful, victorious

Zāharā: shining, luminous

Zāhidā: abstinent

Zāhirā: obvious

Zahrā: white, flowers

Zaidā: fortunate

Zairā: visitor, rose

Zākirā: one who remembers Allah regularly

Zakulā: intelligent

Zameelā: companion

Zamrud: narrator of the Hadith

Zaqirā: witty

Zareenā: companion of Prophet Mohammed

Zarqā: blue

Zaynā: great

Zaynāb: Prophet Mohammed's daughter

Zaytoon: olive

Zuleika: fair-haired

Zulemā: peace